THE ILLUSION OF RETURN

THE ILLUSION OF RETURN

A novel
by
Samir El-Youssef

HALBAN
LONDON

First published in Great Britain by
Halban Publishers Ltd.
22 Golden Square
London W1F 9JW
2007

www.halbanpublishers.com

A CIP catalogue record for this book is available from the
British Library.

ISBN-10: 1 905559 01 1
ISBN-13: 978 1 905559 01 5

Typeset by Computape Typesetting, North Yorkshire
Printed in Great Britain by Mackays of Chatham
a member of The CPI Group

For Linda Grant

1 - Prologue from the essay

I Prologue from the Present

Since the start of this month I have been waiting for the day of the 27th. The closer it gets, the more I have become aware of the fact that it will soon be exactly fifteen years since I left Lebanon. I have been here for fifteen years, that's fifteen years without ever going back, nor seeing any of the people that I used to know then, I kept telling myself with an unmistakable sense of achievement.

You see, over the years I have achieved very little, so little in fact that I was desperate enough to consider an achievement the mere completion of fifteen years without seeing anybody from the past. And now even that sense of achievement turned out to be premature. A short phone call has changed things. It was a call from Ali, an old friend of mine who had left Lebanon two years before I did.

"It's me, Ali, phoning you from America!" he said and told me that on Tuesday the 24th he would be going back to Lebanon, but would be stopping at Heathrow for a couple of hours.

I was quite surprised to hear Ali's voice, and I thought it would be interesting to see him after all these years. Yet I was tempted to tell him that I was going to be busy until the 28th. But I remained silent.

"Goddamit man! It's me, Ali!" he said in a joyful tone of voice. "It's me, Ali phoning you from America, man!"

Having received no immediate reply from me, he must have assumed that I hadn't known who was speaking. And he kept repeating it: "It's me Ali, man!"

I was annoyed and couldn't help asking: "If you are really Ali why the hell are you speaking like that?"

He burst out laughing and instantly switched to Arabic. He didn't realise that it was the accent, not the English, that had annoyed me.

"I would've preferred to meet you at Hajj Ramadan's café," he said amusingly, trying to remind me of the regular meetings that we once had at that café back in Lebanon.

"It must've closed down a long time ago!" I said, and I didn't feel comfortable that he started to talk as if we were still the same friends from the old days.

"No man, it's still there. Only Hajj Ramadan has retired," he said switching back to English.

"How do you know that?" I asked and thought that perhaps he had already been back to Lebanon.

"I am kept informed, man!" he said and went on giving me recent news about people I used to know.

"Yes, fine!" I interrupted him. "What time do you expect to be at Heathrow?"

"One o'clock," he said and went on repeating: "God-damit man, I am talking to you from America!"

"Fine, I'll meet you in Arrivals!" I said hastily trying to end the call.

"We'll see you man!" he replied with a full-of-happiness tone of voice.

Now I can no longer wait for the day of the 27th, I thought putting the receiver down. But I was not sorry. Deep down I had known that anticipating that day was merely an attempt to think of something complete in my life.

I have always yearned for completeness, complete pro-

4

jects, and complete journeys, and as I grew to look at it in an abstract form, complete circles too. It is all quite understandable, given that I have never completed anything in my life. Since as far back as I can remember, everything that I have done or tried to do has been half finished. In recent years I have had a half relationship with a woman, no more than part-time jobs, and I have abandoned my PhD. Thinking about things now, just after I received that call from Ali, I realised that even the chosen topic of my dissertation reflected my obsession with completion.

It was on the Palestinian refugees in Lebanon, and it was meant to depict the end of one state and the beginning of another for a generation of that community. I wanted to show how, due purely to changes in social circumstances, Palestinians had managed to move from the state of an underclass, to which they as refugees had been doomed, to a state in which, socially, if not legally or politically, they were considered middle class. I was particularly excited about it because the emphasis was more on the end than the beginning. But naturally, I didn't complete it. It was one of the things that I really wanted to complete for different reasons, one of which was to spite those who had tried to stop me. At one time I actually vowed to do so as a way of revenge.

When I had decided on this topic I knew that writing such a dissertation might annoy some Palestinians, but I never expected to be ambushed and beaten. Three students who belonged to an organisation that called itself "The Campaign for the Right of Return" attacked me as I was leaving the School of Oriental and African Studies late one evening, just before the Christmas break. To be fair, they had tried to reason with me at first. They came to see me twice and tried to convince me that such a dissertation could serve nobody but those who didn't want to recognise our people's rights.

I was sitting in the Student Union bar when they came to see me the first time. Standing in front of my table, they politely introduced themselves and asked me if we could have a chat. At the beginning I thought they wanted to recruit me into their organisation. I couldn't help feeling surprised. I had never been a member of any organisation or group, nor did I think that any organisation or group would want me to be a member of theirs. What on earth can I offer such people, least of all the "Right of Return" organisation? I thought they were in for a shock the moment they knew my views on the right of return and any such stupidities, and I couldn't help feeling sorry for them. But it turned out that they were well aware of my views: they had heard from other students about my dissertation.

"Quite a few Palestinians have been talking about it," one of them said.

"Really?" I replied, amazed and happily flattered.

"Yes!" he said, though he didn't look in the least impressed.

They then tried to explain to me that such a dissertation would serve nobody but those who didn't want to recognise our people's rights.

I did not understand whom they meant, but one of them volunteered to spell it out to me: "Our – Zionist –

enemy! It would serve nobody but our Zionist enemy!" he said, pronouncing every word distinctly.

"Our Zionist enemy!" I exclaimed and burst out laughing.

They were surprised and annoyed and one of them shouted at me: "What's so funny? Do you think this is funny?"

"No! No!" I hastened to reply, trying to stifle the laughter that had taken hold of me. "It's just I haven't heard this expression for a long time!"

"What?" he shouted at me.

"Our Zionist enemy!" I repeated and couldn't help laughing again. I actually kept repeating these words "Our Zionist enemy", and laughing, which was embarrassing enough to bring our first meeting to an abrupt end. My giggles attracted the attention of other students in the bar and my companions felt awkward and left at once.

But what made it even more amusing was that I was sitting there laughing with four pints of beer in front of me. You see, when these guys turned up to see me, I thought that since we were going to have a serious talk we must have a drink too. So I went to the bar and bought each of us a pint, but I soon discovered that they didn't drink.

"We don't touch alcohol!" one of them informed me proudly.

"I see!" I said, and found myself left with four pints waiting to be drunk.

It was a laughable situation even before they mentioned the words "Our Zionist enemy", and by the time I had finished the fourth pint this expression had become the funniest joke I had ever heard. They had disappeared from the campus by then, and I thought that I had seen the last of them, but obviously they didn't want to give up on me so easily.

Two days later they came back. Wisely, this time we met in the canteen not in the bar. Again they tried to prove to me that my dissertation could do us Palestinians nothing but harm. And though they, wisely too, refrained from using the expression, "Our Zionist enemy", they did not succeed in changing my mind.

"Can't you understand our point?" one of them shouted at me in the voice of a desperate man.

"I do understand," I said. Nevertheless I could not accept their argument.

It was not that they didn't argue well, it was the rhetoric which they used. Somehow I felt that such rhetoric belonged to a world to which I no longer related. It belonged to the world of the past, which had increasingly been appearing unreal to me and where people as much as politics were merely parts of a chaotic dream. And that was precisely what I tried to explain to them the second time we met.

"We should be realistic!" I said. "We should be realistic and forget about the idea of the right to return; the only return we should think of is one of a more symbolic value."

But I failed to convince them.

"There's no point in talking to him," one whispered to the other two. They rose at once and left.

A week later, just before the first term break, they attacked me. It was dark and I couldn't see their faces but I knew it was them. I thought of reporting them to the police, but then, I asked myself, what would I have told the police? I was attacked because of the subject of my PhD thesis? And how would I have explained it? I didn't think that the police would have the patience or the sympathy to hear a full explanation. Nobody would, I knew from experience. Explanations of that kind usually took one far away, too far to make sense, even to those who bothered to listen. And probably it was that lack of ability to explain which angered me most and made me vow to complete my dissertation; not only complete it, as I thought to myself in a moment of deep determination, but also to publish it in book form. But I never did finish it. What I didn't fail to do, however, was to get back at those who attacked me.

One day I saw one of their posters on the wall of the corridor that led to the Student Union bar. It was a big poster of a map of mandate Palestine and across it there was the crude slogan: "No Return No Peace!" Below it, in the left corner, was the name of the organisation "The Campaign for the Right of Return". I realised that here was my opportunity to remind them of what I thought of their campaign. Pretending to look at it with great interest, I waited until no one was around, and quickly crossed out the words "the Right of Return", and wrote just above it in capital letters the word WANKERS. And after a moment of hesitation I added an exclamation mark. I turned and hurried away, thinking to myself that they were bound to blame it on "Our Zionist enemy".

I didn't complete my dissertation, and now, after receiving this phone call from Ali, I see that the story of my remaining here without direct contact with anybody from the past is doomed to be yet another incomplete story. But mine was not the only incomplete story, I said to myself with a tinge of consolation, Ali's too was no longer the finished story that I had always entertained.

When Ali left Lebanon seventeen years ago, I, and everybody else who knew him, thought that we would never see him again. He had been an Israeli collaborator, and I thought that he would never return to Lebanon. It was supposed to be a complete story, at least in my mind, that is.

Before Ali left he knew that the Israelis were about to withdraw from the area, and so he made sure that he fled in time. Nearly a month before the Israelis pulled out, he managed to board a plane to Michigan. The way he used to get there made his story more complete. He didn't use the usual route, but the exact opposite. He went to Tel Aviv with the aid of some Israeli acquaintances, obtained an American visa and flew from Ben-Gurion Airport on a one-way ticket. The usual route was closed, the American embassy in Beirut was abandoned, and the airport was in ruins.

He could have travelled through Damascus instead of Tel Aviv, but not without a high risk of being arrested or even shot. The route between our area, which was still under Israeli occupation, and the Syrian border was dominated by different military forces, Syrian, Lebanese and Palestinian, all of which could have arrested Ali for being either an Israeli collaborator or simply a Palestinian, or both. The political situation at that time had reached a level of absurdity that quite often one didn't know who exactly was fighting whom. For instance, Ali could have been arrested by the Syrian forces, or their Lebanese and Palestinian allies, for being an Israeli collaborator and also for being a supporter of Arafat. Arafat was then – for these forces – as much of an enemy as Israel.

Ali knew that he had no other choice than Tel Aviv, we all knew it, but nevertheless it was so curious to see a Palestinian travelling abroad through Israel. It looked as if it was a clear sign of the changing times. But over the years, and though I was well aware of the fact that Ali was living in Michigan, I gradually managed to convince myself that he had never gone there, that he had probably stayed in Israel, and that he had been allowed to settle in the same old village from which his parents had escaped during the war of 1948. It felt like it should be the right ending to Ali's story, the right thing to happen, I thought to myself. And why should Ali and people like Ali not go back there and resume the blocked road of history, I thought to myself at the time, with great enthusiasm. At our second meeting I actually told those buggers from the "Right of Return" organisation about it, but they didn't understand. One of them thought that I was making fun of them.

"Are you saying," he asked me in a sarcastic tone of voice, "that in order for us to achieve our goal of return, we should urge our people to become Israeli collaborators?"

No, I replied seriously, ignoring his sarcasm, and went on to explain that even for someone like me who believed that Palestinian refugees were as practical as any other people, and perhaps even more so, that they should not waste any opportunity to move on – in my imagination, return was the right ending to the story.

I made this announcement and looked at their faces, each one in turn, with the hope that I would be met with looks of approval and appreciation. But no, they didn't seem to understand what I was on about. Nor did they show the slightest interest in further explanation. Nevertheless I thought I must go on explaining. I was excited about that idea and thought it was too good to be left at that. The promised pleasure of articulating it was too tempting for me to fall silent.

"We ought to be realistic and accept that no actual return could ever take place," I started saying and went on for no less than ten minutes. To the credit of my three companions, they listened to me patiently.

"Instead of fooling ourselves into believing in the actual possibility of return," I went on, "we must look at the notion of return as a symbolic value."

I was pleased with the term "symbolic value" so I used it four or five times. For a moment I forgot all about my companions and the ongoing debate and instead thought that such an original idea must have some value, and that perhaps I should have written a long essay on it and got it published in one of those prestigious periodicals. But then

I thought that even if I started writing at that very moment, when I was still excited about the idea, I probably would give up before it was finished. My hand would never go anywhere near the conclusion.

What was more daunting was that the term didn't seem to have any effect on my three listeners. The only thing which actually caught their attention was my earlier statement that we ought to be realistic and forget about an actual return. It seemed that all through my ten minutes' talk they were waiting for me to finish so that they could respond to this very claim.

"Why is it not realistic to demand the right of return?" one of them asked.

I tried to answer him but it seemed that he meant it as a rhetorical question. For without giving me a chance to reply he went on: "Why is it realistic for the Jews to return after two thousand years and it's not realistic for us to return after only fifty years?"

"Have you read Dr Abu Fatta's book on the subject?" asked another and it seemed that it was yet a further rhetorical question, for he soon went on to quote experts and cite surveys which supposedly proved that there was nothing unrealistic about the idea of the right of return.

He looked very pleased with himself, but I didn't really give any consideration to his quotations and surveys. I was upset that none of them had shown enough appreciation of what I was trying to explain, especially the term "symbolic value", and I decided to dismiss whatever they had said as sheer rhetoric.

"Surveys are rubbish," I said. "Any idiot can make a

survey in which he could prove anything he wanted. The whole business of surveys springs from a culture that has very little in common with the culture to which you are trying to apply it."

I went on instructing them in a highly patronising tone: "No survey could ever be entirely objective even if it was sincerely conducted for the sole purpose of objective knowledge."

"But Dr Abu Fatta proves that," the second one replied but I interrupted him saying that Dr Abu Fatta knew shit and went on explaining how truth was determined by cultural context.

"What seems to be an objective truth for you might be considered by the Israelis as sheer propaganda!" I said, and grinned in a way that implied that they still had a lot to learn.

And it worked. They were offended.

"Only a traitor would dare to say what you are saying!" said the first.

"You have no right to speak on behalf of our people," added the second.

"If I were in your place I would have certainly kept my views to myself," the first warned me.

"This kind of talk leads to harm," the second one said in a threatening voice.

But I ignored him. I actually ignored the two who were talking and looked at the third character who had re-mained silent all through the meeting. I hoped to hear him say something different, something intelligent and subtle. To be honest, I was still hoping that he would be the one who would show some consideration for my idea of return as a symbolic value. I thought perhaps that the third one must have chosen to keep silent out of admiration for the originality of my opinion. He must have realised that I was expecting him to say something in my favour. But he didn't, he just gave me a look of contempt, and when nobody was saying anything he stood up, with that look of contempt still on his face, turned and walked away. The other two followed him without hesitation.

Thinking back now, after I have just received that call from Ali, I realise that it was also something to do with accent. For when I looked at the third fellow, I wasn't only expecting him to say something positive about my idea of "symbolic return", but also to hear him, to hear his accent. Deep down I was hoping that he would speak with the same accent as mine. One of the reasons why I didn't take his two friends seriously was not only because of what they were advocating, but also because of their accent. It was the accent which made me feel that we came from two different societies and that what they were saying might have applied to them, but not to me. Unlike Ali and me, and generally people like us who had managed to move from the camp to the city, the three students from the "Right of Return" organisation, or at least the two who were talking to me, spoke with the accent of those who had remained in the camp. In my mind that was the accent of people who were cut off from the world to the extent that they were incapable of being in the least realistic. And that was probably why I started my discussion with them by saying that we must be realistic. I must have assumed, the moment that I heard their accent, that they were going to say something totally unrealistic.

Now, after I have spoken to Ali, I can fully understand how accent might have influenced my reaction to those guys. For example, when Ali said in what sounded like a heavy American accent, "Goddamit man! It's me, Ali!" I couldn't help replying: "If you are really Ali why the hell are you speaking like that?"

I knew he was speaking from America, and it didn't take me more than a few seconds to remember that he had been living there for the last seventeen years. Yet I was annoyed to hear him speaking English with an American accent. And he must have noticed that straight away, for he immediately switched to Arabic. To my relief, and surprise, he spoke it with the same accent that he had seventeen years ago. The English, with the heavy American accent, seemed to have little effect on the way he spoke Arabic.

Yes, it was the accent, I thought after I received Ali's call. The accent of someone who was so flexible and so smooth that after seventeen years he made me recall exactly how things happened; of George and Maher, of himself – Ali – and me, the four of us sitting in Ramadan Café.

Yes it must be the accent, I kept saying to myself as if I was trying to convince myself of that. But then I found myself doubting again. I wondered whether that was enough to make me revive the whole past, which to my surprise, I somehow managed to do. The fact that I came to be so distinctly aware of the reality of individual events and persons, was not the same as knowing for sure that the whole past was real. It must have been something else, I thought. It must have been the fact that this phone call wasn't only from Ali, but from Ali who had been living in America for the last seventeen years, and now he was going back. It was from someone whose life could no longer be treated as a complete story.

Yes, now I can see it exactly, I said to myself, and I was so excited that I couldn't sit still. I thought I would have to go out for a drink, or a walk in the park. This, I thought with increasing excitement, was an original idea, which I had to think through calmly and perhaps write down as an essay or even a small book. I sat at my kitchen table and started to outline the intended essay:

It's a life of a person (Ali) who has been living for seventeen years in a widely stretched world (America) and therefore it cannot be summarised or related in a linear narrative. And that's what makes Ali's life real, and what must have made the past itself reappear so real (at least to me). But how, the question is, could Ali's life in America make the past reappear as real? Here comes the role of the third important fact: Ali's return to a world of the past. By virtue of his life, which couldn't be summarised or related in the form of a linear narrative, Ali manages to enable the past world to acquire some of the characteristics of the real world, and to reappear as such.

I went on rationalising it in this manner. But the more I wrote the less thrilled I became, and by the time I stopped writing I felt sad. I felt sad and frightened. For I could no longer resign myself to the idea that the past was unreal. Now the past had regained an appearance of reality, I thought to myself, and soon an image of Ali, George, Maher and me, the four of us, appeared, sitting at a table in our familiar corner in Ramadan Café.

It must have been some time towards the end of 1982 or the beginning of 1983. We would sit there, talking and smoking, and sipping tea and coffee, till late evening or even midnight, ignoring the fact that there was a curfew. Ali was the centre, playing a vital role in bringing, and keeping, all of us together. For George, Maher and I really had very little in common apart from Ali's friendship. George and Maher despised one another's views and convictions, and I had none.

George at the time was totally absorbed by the philo-sophy of Heidegger, and he thought that Maher's under-standing of things was the result of the crude reasoning one might expect from a Marxist. Maher, on the other hand, considered himself a political activist, and thought that George was no better than any petit-bourgeois in-tellectual who hid from the reality of conflict, or class struggle, as he used to call it, behind a foggy philosophy.

"Fog! Fog!" Maher used to shout out every time George talked about *Dasein* and "Being-in-the-world". The funny thing is that every time Maher shouted out "Fog! Fog!" the owner of the café, Hajj Ramadan, shouted back from his usual corner, "No politics please!"

For Hajj Ramadan believed that every disagreement between us must have been a disagreement over politics.

He forbade people from talking politics in his café, though of course he himself never stopped talking politics. Everybody in Lebanon talked politics, and yet at the same time everybody said that there was no use in talking politics.

George and Maher never agreed with one another. As for me, I never sided with either of them. In fact I had very little interest in what they said. Sometimes I listened out of sheer courtesy, but once the debate became serious and too focused I would stop listening and instead start thinking of somebody else, mostly of Amina.

In those days I was haunted by the image of my sister Amina. She had died ten years earlier, but I couldn't get over my memory of her. It often distracted me and made me unable to talk or listen to other people, and that was probably why both George and Maher paid very little attention to what I thought and believed. Actually there were times when they looked at me as if they were looking at an empty chair. When Ali wasn't there they seemed to hold themselves back from having one of their heated debates. For I often failed to be the worthy audience that they needed in order to have such a debate. It was Ali whom they used to address. He was the best audience they could have hoped for, curious and attentive but never intrusive. He was close to each of them individually, and each thought that he was on their side, and that was what made the debate more exciting for them. Ali pretended to appreciate the depth of George's thoughts, and at the same time he gave Maher the impression that he was just like him, waiting for that revolution whose imminent arrival Maher kept heralding. As for his attitude towards me, he never bothered to pretend. I neither expected him to agree nor even to listen to what I had to say. We were not very close, but our friendship went back years before we knew George and Maher. We were at school together, and together we started smoking, first cigarettes and later joints, and then we started taking pills. Our friends, especially George and Maher, were shocked to know that we took drugs, but we didn't care. We actually tried to encourage them to try them themselves. We enjoyed them and were a bit surprised at how few of our friends took them. Yet whenever we were told off, we used to claim that it was "the situation" that made us need them so badly.

"The situation, you know," Ali and I used to say, "the civil war, and chaos and Israeli occupation!"

"The situation, you know!"

II   The Past

I

It was the last night when Ali, George, Maher and I were together.

That night we were sitting in our usual corner in Ramadan Café, and for nearly forty minutes George tried to explain to us Heidegger's notion of "Being-in-the-world" but failed completely.

"You see, Heidegger is speaking from an ontological concern," George went on, "while you are apparently approaching things from an epistemological point of view." He tried his best to explain the difference between the two approaches and nearly succeeded in gaining our interest but not for long.

"You, along with all western philosophy from Plato till the appearance of Heidegger's book *Being and Time*," George said, in what sounded like a disappointed tone of voice, "have been the victims of the obsession to know the nature of existence and human knowledge. Heidegger, on the other hand, decided to go back to the original question of what we actually mean by Being, in terms of both questions: namely, What is Being? And what do we mean when we ask What's Being?"

Ali and Maher were totally mystified, but I thought that was a reasonable thing to say. Asking what Being meant, I thought, made more sense than asking what the real nature of the world was, or how we knew that it existed. So far so good! I said to myself, but somehow I felt things were gradually getting a little less clear. Eventually I found myself no less mystified than both Ali and Maher. They were not interested anyway.

To be honest, I myself began losing interest half way through. I could no longer give my full attention to George's argument. It was not the first time that such a thing had happened to me. As far back as I could remember, namely since my sister Amina's death, I often found my interest waning whenever conversation tended to be too serious or highly technical. And that particular evening I was overwhelmed with memories of Amina. I had been thinking about her for days, and in fact all that particular day.

It was something my mother said that morning that got me thinking of Amina again, and this time more strongly than usual. Mother was talking about the year in which it snowed when quite innocently she mentioned her: "I think it was the year in which I was pregnant with Amina!" she said, and then fell into a sudden, deep silence.

I understood the cause of her silence at once. It was a long time since I had heard mother speak of Amina. She rarely mentioned her name, and certainly never in front of either father or my brother, Kamal. They had forbidden her to talk about her deceased daughter. Though Kamal had been working in Saudi Arabia, and father had mellowed over the years, mother could never ignore the wishes of either her husband or son. Yet that morning, when mother fell silent after mentioning Amina, I thought that her silence wasn't the result of guilt suddenly seizing her for mentioning a forbidden name. Rather, her silence seemed to stem from her confronting the fact, which up till then must have been relegated to the back of her mind, that Amina, whom she was not permitted to mention, was above all her daughter.

She must have come to face the fact that Amina was her flesh and blood, I said to myself with a slight sense of vindication. All of a sudden she must have realised that Amina was someone whom she bore inside her own body. She must have realised that the bond that tied them together was greater than the one that tied Amina to either father or Kamal.

Of course, I knew that mother might never have had such a thought, but I hoped that she had done, and I couldn't stop thinking of Amina all day and into the night. Thinking of Amina was probably what made me unable to follow what George was saying even though I wanted to. But then, there was also the little matter of the drugs that Ali and I had taken before we went to the café. We didn't take them in order to become deaf to George's explanation of the difference between the ontological and the epistemological approaches nor indeed what "Being-in-the-world" meant. We took them simply because we thought they were a good kind of drug. We called them "the pills of happiness", and they were meant to make us relaxed, yet without being dull and stupid at the same time. We had bought them from a pharmacist who didn't mind selling drugs without prescription so long as he was well paid for them.

"I promise you that these pills will make you extremely relaxed," the pharmacist assured us, "so relaxed, in fact, you will tolerate anybody, including those who would curse your parents."

25

Ali and I were happy that they would make us relaxed, but were not sure that tolerating those who cursed our parents somehow was proof of a good effect.

"Actually we don't need any pills to tolerate such people," Ali replied, but the pharmacist took it as a joke and went on explaining the side-effects of the pills. He sounded as if he was trying to prove to us that he had studied pharmacology, and the fact that he was selling us drugs without prescription didn't make his scientific qualifications any less valid. We, however, were not interested in all he wished to say, but nevertheless we had to be polite and listen to him patiently.

"After all, he's our only supplier at the moment," Ali said after we left the pharmacist.

"Yes, unfortunately," I said, and couldn't help remembering our old supplier, Bassem.

He was a real pusher, good and reliable, but the Resistance had killed him a few weeks earlier. Ali and I were sad about his death. But we were also surprised that the Resistance had picked on him in particular. Most people were surprised and some wondered whether he was an Israeli collaborator as well as a drug pusher. Why would the Resistance kill Bassem if he weren't a collaborator? That's what people wondered. And they thought that the Resistance had done well by any account. He was, after all, a drug pusher too, people said with a clear sense of self-righteousness.

"People are just being hypocrites," Ali said when we discussed the matter later on in the café.

"They usually are!" I said.

"Perhaps they are hypocrites," Maher objected, "but you can't deny the fact that this time they are right. Anyway he must've been a collaborator!"

"How do you know?" I asked with annoyance.

"How do I know?" he repeated my question with a sense of astonishment, "I know, I just know!"

"How?" I asked and I was getting more annoyed.

"Well, I shan't reveal all the information I have at the moment," he replied, "but I can assure you that the Resistance is far too busy fighting the occupation and its collaborators to start chasing drug pushers!"

"Balls!" I exclaimed.

"Balls?" he replied, "you don't know what you're talking about. And anyway I hope you didn't blab too much in front of him."

Maher was worried about himself, or so he pretended. He used to claim that he was working for the Resistance but that was a secret, he warned us, which should never go beyond our small circle. We, especially Ali and I (for George rarely showed any interest in such matters), didn't believe that he worked for the Resistance. And we thought that he wouldn't mind it a bit if the whole world suspected he was in the Resistance. After all, why would he bother spreading such a rumour if it weren't for the obvious risk he faced of being arrested by the Israelis, or, worse still, being kidnapped by their collaborators.

"I hope you didn't mention my name in front of him!" Maher berated us again.

Soon, however, it turned out that Bassem was not a collaborator, and that the Resistance had executed him because he was a drug dealer. Like most of us Maher was surprised, and couldn't conceal his slight disappointment. He did not expect the Resistance to worry about drug pushers when we faced, as he used to say, a greater enemy, the Israeli occupation and its henchmen. But instead of expressing his sense of surprise and disappointment, as Ali and I did in rather loud voices, he hastened to justify the killing.

"The role of the Resistance is not only to fight the military occupation and its collaborators, but also to deal with many social ills," he said looking at us.

"Balls!" Ali and I replied at once.

"No, it's not balls," he protested, "there is no point in liberating society from its political enemies, and doing nothing about its social enemies!"

"Social enemies!" Ali replied. "You call that poor sod Bassem a social enemy?"

"To you he might have been only a poor sod," Maher explained impatiently, "but objectively speaking he was . . . "

"Here he goes again," Ali interrupted, "fucking objectively speaking! What does that mean?"

"Yes, objectively speaking your poor sod was a parasite who was delaying the coming revolutionary change."

Ali fell silent for a minute. He couldn't simply dismiss what was called revolutionary change as utter nonsense too – even though, as I gathered, that was precisely what he wished to do. He had always agreed with Maher that nothing should block the way of revolutionary change and progress, and now he had to agree that Bassem, of all people, was standing in the way.

It serves him right, I said to myself and could not help grinning. And he must have noticed my grin and realised what I was thinking.

"And should the Resistance chase thieves and prostitutes and adulterers and queers?" he returned to question Maher, and I could not help noticing that he pronounced the word "queers" with a sense of unease. It was understandable, I thought. For it was known that Ali's brother Sameh was a homosexual. We pretended not to know, so as not to embarrass Ali. Ali was not stupid, but he was grateful that none of us said anything about Sameh. Nevertheless whenever one of us used the word homosexual, a look of embarrassed awareness crept over his face, and he gazed suspiciously at the person who mentioned it as if to see whether he was referring to his brother. But this time it was he who said it, and in spite of the unease that he felt, he hastened to question Maher in a way that felt as if he was trying to forget that he had mentioned the word "queers".

"How about all of them? Aren't they objective enemies? Shouldn't the Resistance kill them all as well?" he asked in an unusually angry tone. And I felt that this anger was a reflexive response to the sudden embarrassment he felt.

"Yes, they are all social enemies, and should be dealt with!" Maher said firmly, as if to imply that no matter how Ali felt, he would not change his view out of mere compassion for him.

Ali shook his head in disbelief, and turned towards

George as if he were seeking his help. Not that he expected George to challenge Maher on this very issue, for George was extremely cautious not to get involved in a political debate of this kind. Nevertheless Ali wanted to change the subject, and change it in such a way that would annoy Maher, and George was uniquely capable of doing just that. George would raise philosophical issues while Maher would get irritated and start interrupting him, either by shouting out "Fog! Fog!" or by trying to dispute every statement that he made.

And that evening when George tried, and failed, to explain to us what Heidegger meant by "Being-in-the-world", Maher actually was one of the reasons for George's failure.

"Fog! Fog!" he kept crying out, interrupting George who was really trying to make things as clear as possible.

"Totally irrelevant to what concerns us here!" he said, and later repeated a few times, especially when he realised that George was gaining our attention.

Maher didn't like it when we paid attention to George and he often tried to interfere and dispute what George was saying. Nevertheless, he thought that he was doing us a favour by making it difficult for George to persuade us. He believed that Ali and I were a pair of fools who could easily be swayed one way or the other. And therefore, it was his "revolutionary duty", as he once told us, being a revolutionary activist, to shield us from the danger of petit-bourgeois thinking which, according to him, George was spreading. He also hoped that he would be able to recruit us into serving the Resistance, or at least help him in some of his most urgent duties.

Years later, when Ali and I met for a few hours at Heathrow airport, we remembered how serious Maher had been back then. We thought that it would have been interesting to know what kind of a mission he intended to assign to us.

"Perhaps gathering information behind enemy lines!" Ali said in English.

"A mission similar to the one he was carrying out, more like it!" I said, referring sarcastically to the fact that Maher had nothing to do with the Resistance.

"He was a loser, man!" Ali said in English.

"Perhaps . . . but a harmless loser," I said in English too.

"Yeah," Ali said, and added after a pause, "he destroyed himself in the end."

"Anybody could tell that he meant no harm," I said, switching back to Arabic. Those last two sentences had aroused such painful memories I was unable to continue that playful conversation in English.

We had just started talking about the past, and we kept referring to various pleasant and casual memories. Neither of us had the courage to dig deep right away, and recall those painful events of that last night which tore us apart. We knew that eventually we would talk about those events, but up till that moment we were content to remember harmless details. And there certainly were plenty of those to recall, especially when it came to that endless contest between Maher and George.

"He hated George!" Ali said, reminding me of how

31

Maher used to interrupt George all the time.

"He wanted to protect us!" I said.

He wanted to protect us, true enough, I thought. But that was not the only reason why he kept giving George a hard time. He actually disliked George. He couldn't make head or tail of him.

"I don't understand what use George has for Heidegger's philosophy, or any other philosophy for that matter," he used to complain when George was absent. Predictably, he often enough accused George of being a useless intellectual who kept hiding from reality behind a smoke screen of philosophy. George was nevertheless our friend, and in the actual terms of our daily speech an accusation such as "petit-bourgeois intellectual" meant very little. Maher then started thinking that George must have been "up to something".

"I think that he speaks about such lofty concepts in order to impress you, and then use you for his own purposes," he said once.

Maher was in the habit of suspecting that there was always a purpose, and invariably a sinister one, for whatever people did, or didn't do.

"If I have learned anything at all from studying Lenin," he told us once, "it is that nothing is done purposelessly or innocently." But we knew that he did not need Lenin to teach him such a thing. He always liked to attribute dubious purposes and intentions to people, and consequently labelled them as either anarchists or reactionaries or "objective enemies of the revolution". He could not help labelling people, especially those who were not of his revolutionary creed. But when he eventually realised that George had no intention of using us, he was surprised and somehow disappointed. And then confused. The fact that George had no practical purpose for his philosophy made it difficult for Maher to label him an "objective enemy of the people". Finally he had no other option but to add him to the list of those who didn't care one way or another.

"A nihilist! That's what he is!" he exclaimed bitterly and in a tone which implied that it hurt him deeply to acknowledge such a regrettable yet inescapable fact.

Maher and George had had their usual debate about the role of intellectuals in the world. George insisted that it was premature to assume that the intellectual had a role before they had resolved "the essential question of Being".

"Balls!" said Maher. "In fact, balls to the purpose which is only to distract the working class from its mission!"

"Which working class?" This time it was I who objected, while George fell silent. And it wasn't often that I objected and then only when he started to talk about classes that did not exist.

"Don't keep asking that question," he replied impatiently. "You don't know what you are talking about!"

"There is no working class in this country, is there?" I pointed out. "There is no industry, no factories," I said and added sarcastically, after a moment's hesitation, "apart from the one that comrade Salim blew up!"

I burst out laughing as I said that. Both Ali and George

joined me while Maher cried out in anger: "Nihilists! You are all nihilists!" And from his usual corner behind the till, Hajj Ramadan shouted back his familiar mantra: "No politics, please!"

And that night when the four of us were together for the last time, Maher was determined to prove to us that George was a nihilist. So he kept on interrupting:

"Being-in-the-world!" he repeated sarcastically. "Being-in-the-fucking-world more like it!"

George tried to ignore him, but Maher kept on and on. "And how does that help us fight Israeli occupation?" he asked in a voice loud enough to be heard not only by the owner of the café, but also by passers-by in the street. Naturally, instead of expecting an answer to such a question, we fell silent waiting for Hajj Ramadan to shout from his corner: "No politics, please!"

"Tell me, how does Heidegger help us fight the Israeli occupation? Huh? Tell me!" repeated Maher, but in a whisper this time.

Undaunted, George ignored him and went on to explain the difference between ontological and epistemical perspectives. Maher shook his head in disbelief. He could not understand why George had no interest in such an important question. Of course Maher didn't actually expect to get an answer from George. He knew very well that George didn't talk politics, that no matter what was said and how it was said, George had no interest in politics, especially politics in Lebanon. Maher, however, never understood why George didn't talk politics, especially when everyone else did. And he took it as further proof that George was a nihilist.

Maher was not the only one who failed to understand George's lack of interest in politics. Ali and I often wondered about this too, but never managed to get anywhere near a satisfactory explanation. What we failed to realise was that in spite of his lofty intellectual pursuits, George was following the example of his family – his father, mother, brother and sister who never showed the slightest interest in politics. They believed that if they stayed out of politics altogether, none of the rival political factions and groups, which dominated the area, could consider them as enemies. They were Christian Palestinians with Lebanese citizenship who lived in an area dominated largely by Moslems, both Lebanese and Palestinian. Steering away from politics – that is, proving that they had no political alliance – must have helped them avoid being harassed by local militias of various persuasions, I thought. But they were never completely safe, and on a few occasions George's father and brother were kidnapped and beaten. Once or twice armed men knocked at their door and told them that they should leave the area if they knew what was good for them. There was also a time when someone tried to set fire to their apartment in the night while they were asleep. It was at the beginning of the civil war, and a man whose brother had died in the fighting in Beirut sought revenge on them, as one of the few Christian families in the area. He poured petrol under the front door but luckily for them he was caught before he managed to strike a match. Of course they thought of leaving the area but they had nowhere else to go, and besides, war was breaking out in different parts of the country and nobody was sure any longer which part was still safe.

And that night, the last night when the four of us were together, Maher tried hard to drag George into a political debate. I had the feeling that he would have tried even harder had Ali remained, but there was no point in having such a debate without him.

Just as curfew time was approaching, Ali's youngest brother came to the café and told him that he was wanted urgently. We were worried, and tried to find out what the urgent matter was, but Ali hastened to reassure us, saying that it was probably nothing. Most likely his parents only wanted to scare him so that he would go home before the curfew, he joked. Ali left and the confrontation between Maher and George came to an end. They resorted to the sort of conversation which they often had whenever Ali was not there. There was no longer a worthy audience in front of which they would try to outdo one another. They suspected that I was not going to pay them the same attention that Ali usually did. They were right, because the moment Ali left I even dispensed with my half interested attitude, which I had maintained all through the evening. I stopped listening to them and started thinking of Amina again. I had thought of Amina for days on end, and on that evening in particular, I was waiting for Ali to leave so I could be free to think of my sister. For some reason I often found it hard to think of her when Ali was around. It was as if Ali could read my mind and know what I was thinking. He knew my family and was aware of

Amina's tragic death; he knew how ashamed my parents felt every time someone mentioned her, though they, and my brother Kamal, had always maintained that Amina's death was the result of an accident. He also knew that I had never managed to get over it. On the few occasions when he and I talked about it, I could not help crying, while he felt embarrassed.

And that night, after Ali left, and as if to celebrate my sudden freedom to think about her, I started wondering: had Amina lived, what sort of a man would she have wanted to fall in love with and marry? Take, for example, these two companions of mine, George and Maher. Who would she have chosen? I hoped that she would have chosen George. Unlike Maher, he was subtle and had depth, trying to justify my own choice for her. But in truth that was not the only reason for preferring George. I hoped to see her defying everybody once again, and marrying a Christian. I thought the whole family, aunts and uncles and cousins, would be outraged. "Our daughter marrying a Christian! Has she no shred of shame left?" they would say. I could just imagine it and felt satisfied.

But I assumed that, regrettably, George would probably offer to convert to Islam in order to be rid of the problem. I hoped that Amina wouldn't allow him to do so. I fancied that she would choose to run away with him, to Germany or America. I tried to imagine the attitude of my parents and Kamal and the whole family. What could they have done worse than they already had? I asked myself. They had disowned her, they permitted no mention of her name, and I expected that some uncles and aunts would also ban her name from conversation, though only in front of my parents and Kamal. Amongst themselves, however, they would mention her all the time, not out of grief and guilt, but out of small-minded vindictiveness. They would refer to her as a shameful example who should be avoided. "Don't do what Amina did!" one aunt would tell her daughters time and again; or "What! Do you intend to follow Amina's example and bring upon us a new shame?"

Amina, I thought, would forever remain in their eyes a cursed person. But I myself would defy them all, I said to myself, just as Amina had done. I would mention her with admiration, and I might even try to get in touch with her wherever she happened to be. I would write to her, telling her what was going on. But most importantly, I would ask her about her life with George. I even imagined myself impatiently waiting for her letters and postcards.

Yes, that night after Ali had left and I found myself sitting alone with George and Maher, I thought of Amina in an unusual way. I dreamt of her running away with George, whom I had judged the better choice of the two. But then I looked at George again, and wondered if I was right after all. Amina would not have liked him either, I thought. She was a realistic, practical woman, while George was too obscure to be realistic and too comfortable in his abstract thinking to be practical. Amina, I thought, would have regarded him as being as useless as Maher; the pair of them were all talk and no deed. I remembered how active Amina was, how she used to be totally involved in her work with the Women's Organisation to which she belonged. Sometimes she would leave home early in the morning and not return before midnight. She was always on the go, supervising the production of leaflets and preparation for public meetings and workshops.

I recalled the image of Amina as she really was, and when I resumed listening to George and Maher, I knew she would have thought they were no more than a pair of chatterers. And she would have been right! There they are, I said to myself, bored of debating and arguing, but instead of seeking to know the cause of that boredom, they go on trying to reach a point at which neither could be declared a winner. Listening to them, I knew that without a worthy audience, they were bound to be bored. Nevertheless, there was still the sense of satisfaction that they had participated in a philosophical debate that only a handful of people could have understood.

I listened to them and knew that each one of them would soon retreat to his own final words of wisdom. Maher, on the one hand, would remind George of what Marx had said, that philosophers had wasted their precious time trying to interpret the world, thus neglecting the real task of changing it; while George, on the other, would give him that look which said "What a pair of morons you are, both Marx and you!" And he would return to his usual assertion that it was pointless to try to change something when one did not understand what it was in the first place. Indeed, George would assert that it was premature even to suggest that the world needed change before one knew what Being-in-the-world was. And certainly, one should know what was meant by Being itself. Of course Maher wouldn't want to leave it at that, but obviously he would be too tired to respond and indeed George himself would look too tired to listen to further responses. He seemed willing to admit that what he had just said didn't actually refute Marx's claim, but rather tended to postpone its truth. Yet despite that apparent concession, Maher would lack the energy even to look gratified or relieved. And eventually they would both fall silent, bored and wearily silent.

2

It was the last night when the four of us were together.

That night George and I decided to take a stroll after Maher and Ali had left the café. There was a curfew and we knew that it was time to leave, but neither of us wished to go home straight away. We felt so restless that we were actually willing to risk being arrested, or even shot at, rather than go home. We said goodnight to Hajj Ramadan who was taking his money out of the till and counting it, and then we stepped out.

It was totally dark and nobody was to be seen anywhere. This had always been the case in the area, even before the Israeli invasion of Lebanon in 1982 and the subsequent constant rule of curfew. Of course now it had become even more dangerous, particularly for the likes of us. Israeli collaborators were often on the lookout for Palestinians, or Lebanese with left-wing sympathies. Picking on Palestinians and left-wing Lebanese was the way the collaborators imposed their power in the area. But some of them also sought revenge for relatives or friends who had been harassed and expelled from the area before 1982, when it was still under the control of Palestinian factions and left-wing militias.

George and I were well aware of the risk that we were taking, but the anticipation of danger seemed merely an additional motive for our late venture. What made it more surprising for me was to see George, of all people, willing to stroll around at that time of night and in those circumstances.

Yes, it was surprising to see George, I thought, the same George who used to refrain from expressing a political opinion for no other purpose than to stay out of trouble. At the time I couldn't bring myself to imagine him being arrested or kidnapped. I nearly asked him if he would rather go home, but he looked quite determined, certainly more determined than I was.

It was both surprising and funny. It seemed as if he were enjoying the fact that we were choosing to be out in the streets at precisely that time of night. Normally it wasn't safe for people like us to be out even during the day, so one could imagine how dangerous it was at night. It must have given George a refreshing sense of being different – different not only from the people of the city, but also from the rest of humanity. At least it encouraged him, and me, to say things that we would never have thought of expressing at any other time. And that was what I remembered when I recalled the events of that evening years later, that we both said things that we would not have imagined ourselves talking about in ordinary times. Luckily for me, the only thing I dared say was to make the silly suggestion of opening a café for talking philosophy. George was astonished and looked at me to see whether I was joking.

"Yes, a café," I said, "a place where people can meet and talk philosophy."

"Are you serious?"

"Yes!" I said. "There should be a place where people can meet and talk solely in abstract terms."

"In abstract terms?" he repeated my words, looking at

42

me as if he were seeing me for the first time in his life. I ignored his look and went on explaining that in that proposed café of mine there should be a rule that no conversation should be based on personal or collective prejudice, nor should it refer to historical facts. "Purely abstract concepts and terms – that's all that would concern us!" I announced.

George kept gazing at me with the look of someone who was more surprised than curious. He was probably thinking of something to say in response, something which I assumed would show me how devastatingly stupid my idea was. Yet he remained silent, and for a while I thought I'd better change the subject. George had no interest in my frivolous ideas, I thought. He probably assumed that I had made that suggestion for no other purpose than to arouse his curiosity, and that was why he rightly decided to ignore it. Perhaps I should say something to assure him that the idea of such a café was not made on the spur of the moment. Perhaps I should tell him that I had been thinking about it for a long time, precisely since we had been having all those earlier philosophical debates and that might please him. Yet still I said nothing, and it was he who eventually broke the silence.

"But you know," he said in a tone of voice which sounded as if he was deep in thought, "to talk in purely abstract concepts, as you put it, is to end in silence!"

"Why?" I asked, and felt happy that, at last, he had decided to take my suggestion seriously. "Can't we maintain a debate in abstract terms?"

"You see, if an expression is to be totally abstract, if it is to be something that's totally separated from reality and history, then it would return to its origin and die," he said.

George gave me a look as if to urge me to ask him what he had meant. He must have realised that I didn't understand his meaning; however he himself was not going to explain it voluntarily. That was something which George often enjoyed doing. He would make a complicated statement and, instead of simplifying it, he would fall into a calculated silence. It was not that he particularly enjoyed baffling his listeners – only that he seemed to like the idea of a statement being something of a mystery. For him, I thought, such a mystery must have been a sign, or a reminder, of those many things in our lives which could never be fully explained. And for a minute or two I was tempted to go along with his wish and refrain from seeking an explanation.

On the other hand, I was worried that George might think that I was not interested. I was also worried that my remaining silent might lead me back to the state of half-interest to which I had often drifted. The suggestion of opening a café was, as I realised later, nothing if not an attempt to get myself into a good conversation. I had thought that if I made conversation, instead of being a mere listener to one initiated and taken up by others, I might be able to give my full attention to it. George himself didn't fail to notice that I was trying to be completely engaged, and quite understandably he looked amused. He didn't believe that I was capable of being more than half-interested, and probably suspected that I was feigning the enthusiasm which I had shown. But I wasn't pretending, and, in fact, it was extremely difficult for me to focus on what either he or we were talking about.

On the rare occasions when I forced myself to be fully attentive, I felt as if I had been locked up in a room which had no door or window or any kind of exit at all. The whole attempt was such a claustrophobic ordeal that I swore never to repeat it. But that night, after we had left the café and walked through the dark and deserted streets of the city, ignoring the imposed state of curfew, I thought there must be very little that I was not willing to do, including being able to focus on what was being said. I thought that I must be attentive to my companion, and apart from that, I actually wanted a conversation in which I could fully participate.

George himself seemed keen to show his appreciation for my unusual attitude. Instead of waiting for me to ask what he had meant when he said that abstract talk could only lead to silence, he voluntarily went on explaining: "Remember what happened to Descartes! How in seeking a kind of pure and irrefutable knowledge, he ended where he had started from, the abstract self, or the 'thinking thing' as he called it."

"Descartes was a fool," I replied without knowing exactly why I said such a thing. I probably wanted to show him my total understanding of the argument.

"That might've been the case," he said quite seriously, "but his attempt shows that if all empirical knowledge and every concrete perception were disregarded, then the abstract self is the only thing that is left for us. And that's not much to go on."

"Yes! Yes!" I replied.

"Descartes," George continued, "proved, without any doubt, the existence of the abstract self, but nothing else beyond, and therefore his meditation led him to nothing but silence."

And as if to illustrate the point he was making, George himself promptly fell silent.

"He tried to bring in God to get out of this difficulty," I hastened to say, trying, first, to prove to him that I was well aware of what he was talking about, and at the same time, to make sure that the conversation continued. His sudden silence made me a bit wary.

"It was a hopeless attempt," said George, and added in a matter-of-fact tone, "there is no God!"

I was a bit startled to hear him making such a statement, especially in such a casual manner. I was never religious; none of my family were, apart from my brother Kamal who had only turned to religion after he had gone to Saudi Arabia. Yet I felt startled and so uneasy hearing George deny the existence of God with such effortlessly expressed words. Denying the existence of God, I had always thought, should be made as a more challenging form of expression; it should be inciting and noisy, and not just as a matter of fact.

I decided to object to what George had said, to tell him that he could not deny the existence of God as simply as he did, that the notion of God was too important to be dismissed without paying attention to the challenge it posed. "I am not a believer," I said with some hesitation trying to find the best way to convey my uneasiness, "but you cannot . . . "

"Why not?" he interrupted calmly. "If you are not a believer and I'm certainly not, then why give the thought of God any attention at all?"

"Yes, but there are many people who believe in God," I protested.

"Gullible people, idiots frightened of uncertainty!" he said impatiently. Though after a while, he added calmly: "We cannot avoid silence by talking about the existence of that which doesn't exist!"

I assumed that he made this additional statement because he thought that the reason why I had objected to his offhand denial of the existence of God was my fear of ending the conversation in a sudden and long silence.

"But it's not only the fear of silence!" I hastened to reply, as if to prove to him that my earlier objection genuinely had gone beyond our present conversation. Then, I hadn't been frightened of silence: I wanted him to understand that and decided to say no more.

We were both silent, but not for long. It seemed that the danger which we had anticipated appeared sooner than we had expected. The sound of an approaching vehicle filled the street, and I had no doubt that it was an Israeli military vehicle.

Startled, I looked in different directions trying to find a way to escape or, at least, a place in which to hide. There was an alleyway a few steps from where we were, through which we could run to an adjacent street and from there, in the opposite direction to the vehicle, make our way home. Or perhaps we could hide in a porch of one of the houses which stretched along the alleyway.

"Come on!" I urged George pointing to the alleyway and running.

George didn't move. He stood still looking towards the source of the sound, waiting calmly for the vehicle to appear.

"Come on, for God's sake!" I shouted at him. I was overcome with fear, and the thought that he was so close to being caught by an Israeli patrol made me angry too. "For God's sake, man!" I shouted again.

Still he didn't move. Instead he looked at me with that same calm look of his, and said: "I told you, I don't believe in God!"

"Forget about that shit now!" I said trying to hurry him to escape. "We must hide!"

And I ran, hoping that he would be encouraged to follow me. I stopped in the middle of the alleyway and started calling for him. I called three or four times, in a low voice this time, fearing that the Israeli patrol had come close enough to hear any shouting. Eventually I had to give up and hide in a doorway.

What the fuck is he playing at? I asked myself in great panic, and thought that soon the Israelis would see him and arrest him. I wondered what my next move should be in that case. I was well aware of how little could be done if he was arrested. I knew of nobody who could plead with the Israelis on his behalf – no one who could explain to them that he was a totally harmless person. Perhaps it was possible that George's family would be able to talk to some of the Christian militias, who were loyal to Israel, I thought. Yet deep down I knew that there was no such possibility. They knew nobody who had influence and authority: they seemed incapable of knowing anybody who could help them in the case of their own son being arrested.

What the fuck is he playing at? I asked myself. Anger started to replace my fear for him, and even my fear for myself. Perhaps the mad bastard deserved to be arrested and taken to Ansar Prison for a few months, I said to myself. So I just waited there, listening carefully. To my relief I realised that the sound of the vehicle was slowly disappearing. The Israeli patrol seemed to have taken a different route. I left my hiding place but remained in the alleyway until I was sure that the vehicle had disappeared completely.

Of course I was waiting to get back to George and show him how angry I was. But then realising that the danger had passed, I didn't know what to say, what expression to use. To shout and swear at him, to make fun of him, to tell him that what he had done was not heroic but irrespon-sible, to tell him that he had been both irresponsible and selfish, that he had no consideration for me, for his friends or parents?

No, I couldn't say such things to him. I remembered that I didn't know him well enough to be able to say any of that, or even to reproach him in any way. After all, I thought, he was a person with whom just five minutes earlier I had been struggling to keep a conversation going. George was actually a stranger to me.

And when I went back to the street and saw him standing there, waiting for me, I felt bitterly angry – yet I couldn't say a word. I tried to calm down, telling myself that I was bound to find out why he had behaved that way, that he was bound to say something.

Years later, when I met Ali for a few hours at Heathrow Airport, I told him what had happened that night. "I've never understood why George behaved that way," I said. "He was not a particularly brave person. Needless to say, there was no bravery in what he did."

"He was weird, man!" Ali said. "His family was weird too."

"Yes I know!" I said in a way implying that I knew enough about George's family to realise how strange they were.

"Did you know them well?" Ali asked me in Arabic. His immediate switch into Arabic revealed a considerable degree of curiosity.

"I didn't know them well," I said, "but George told me a lot about them!"

"Like what?" Ali asked. I was instantly surprised to see him so curious all of a sudden. We had started talking about the past, but up till that moment he had shown only polite concern about what was being said.

"I wonder what has happened to them," I said trying to ignore his question.

"Nothing, they are still there!" Ali replied directly, as if to make sure that nothing else would be mentioned and to stop me from revealing what I had known.

"In the same apartment?" I asked. "How about George? I bet he's married by now!"

"No he's not!" Ali replied impatiently. "He's still living with his parents in the same apartment."

"What about his brother and sister?" I asked, again trying to avoid telling Ali what he wished to know. Somehow I felt that what George had told me that night when we went out for a stroll was secret; and he meant it to remain a secret, even after so many years. That night George entrusted me with what he had never entrusted anyone else, I thought, and so I decided not to tell Ali anything.

That night after we were nearly captured by the Israeli patrol, we continued our walk silently. This time it was me who very much wanted us to remain silent. I was still angry and was in no mood to resume talking about philosophy or anything else that was meant to be serious. I wanted to make sure that we were heading back home without delay, while George, I realised, wished to continue our stroll and to talk.

"It would be interesting to have a place where debates and conversations could lead to silence," he said, all of a sudden, trying to resume our conversation in a casual way, as if nothing of importance had happened.

He seemed eager to assure me that my idea of opening a café for philosophers was not without its merits. I was still upset, and at that moment felt that I had no use for his appreciation. He would make more sense if he could tell me why he hadn't run away when we heard the Israeli patrol approaching. I nearly said that after what had happened, this was no time to talk philosophy. Instead it was best to go home before we found ourselves facing another Israeli patrol. He wouldn't pay attention to me; at that very moment he was clearly on another planet. I decided to calm down and lead him all the way to the doorstep of his home, and then hurry back to my own. I walked silently until I calmed down, and then looked at him and asked if he had really thought that my idea was worthwhile.

He nodded and went on to explain to me how important it was to discover a language which could lead us to the origin of speech. And such an origin, as he explained, was silence.

"Who knows, perhaps that'd be the only way to shut Maher up!" I interrupted him jokingly.

"Nothing will shut Maher up," he said, "he'll go on talking!"

"Talking is the only way to prove that he exists!" I said and laughed. I felt calm now, and for a moment wondered if I had exaggerated my worry and anger over what had happened earlier. True, I thought, it was wrong of him not to run, but now we could regain our earlier sense of freshness and have a joke at Maher's expense.

"Maher's *cogito* is," I said trying to get George in a joking mood, "I talk therefore I am!"

But he didn't laugh. He remained silent and I assumed that he must have been preparing himself to express something serious about Maher. I always knew that he held an opinion of Maher that informed what he said when debating with him. It was that opinion that often determined when to cease debating with Maher or whether to start a debate in the first place.

"He's lucky, you know," he said all of a sudden.

"Lucky?"

"Yes, people like him are usually lucky. They talk all the time because they are lucky," he said. And after a moment of silence he added: "People like Maher have never had the misfortune of confronting the non-being of Being."

"Does that make him lucky?" I said in a voice that failed to conceal my disappointment. Now that I had calmed down, I was hoping that George would say something straightforward, express a blunt opinion, for example. Maybe he would say that Maher was a pompous intellectual who talked of practical achievements and political commitment to overcome the crude nature of his thinking. But no, I said to myself, George was determined to talk the same way as when we met in the café. The fact that the two of us were alone, that we were walking in the middle of the night through the deserted streets of a city under curfew, that for a moment we were about to be caught by an Israeli patrol – none of that seemed to make enough difference for him to change the language he usually used. He simply could not dispense with expressions such as "the non-being of Being" and similar nonsense expressions, I said to myself, and felt so disappointed that I decided to change the subject altogether. I decided to talk about general things, or anything which would not give him an excuse to use his usual jargon.

I actually thought of leaving him at that very moment, saying goodnight and walking away, and to hell with him returning home safely, I said to myself. Why should I make sure that he's safely home? I thought. So I decided to leave him and go home at the earliest opportunity.

He must have detected how disappointed I was. For instead of continuing to express what he thought of Maher, and people like him, he fell silent. We walked without speaking for more than five minutes. And for a moment I wondered whether by remaining silent, he was trying to apologise to me for not being able to express himself in an open and chatty way. Or perhaps, yet again, he meant to give me a practical demonstration of how talking in abstract terms could lead to nothing but silence. But this time the silence between us was so noticeably tense that even George must have realised that it wasn't merely the result of speaking in abstract terms.

I felt that one of us had to break the silence, otherwise it would impose itself on our friendship forever; indeed, it might determine the fate of such a friendship. If we were to go on silently until the end of our stroll, I thought, then neither of us would ever be interested in speaking to the other again. It would mean that we had nothing left to tell one another, that we had nothing in common.

These few moments felt like a rare encounter, perhaps the only encounter, upon which depended whatever was going to happen between us in the next few days, or even in the distant future. I was also aware that this decisively tense silence was the result of walking in the night in such circumstances. It was highly possible that everything that had taken place would be forgotten the next morning.

He had to break the silence, and so he talked for a long time. Of course he didn't talk about the "non-being of Being" or anything like that. Instead, he spoke about a life without passion or intimacy, his own life. It was a secret. And years later when I met Ali at Heathrow Airport I still thought of this conversation as a secret and decided not to reveal it to Ali.

"I live in a cold home," George said. "As far back as I can remember I've always lived in a home where there is no place for emotions, no anger or rage, yet also, no joy or happiness either."

"No intimacy," I said, trying to assure him that I understood what he was talking about.

This was the first time that George had talked about his family in front of me, or anybody else, as far as I knew. He always made sure that his private life raised neither concern nor curiosity. Whenever he was asked a question about his family he answered in a way that implied there was nothing there worth talking about or even knowing. We never showed too much interest in his family anyway, not only out of respect for his privacy but because we didn't like to talk about our families either. For one reason or another we suffered a shared sense of embarrassment and shame about our own families, especially Ali and me. Ali was ashamed of his brother Sameh, and I kept feeling guilty about my sister Amina. But that was not all. We often wished to be as far away from our parents as possible. Nothing they said or did seemed to command respect or appreciation. We felt ashamed of them and wished to hear as little about them as possible. So that evening when George talked about his family, I couldn't help feeling embarrassed. Of course I was curious to hear him talking about his parents' private life so openly, but embarrassment overcame me and made me wish that he would stop.

I had seldom met George's parents. Nevertheless, on the infrequent occasions when I had, I found them friendly and even warm. George explained that although they did not actually lack emotions, they never showed them either to or in front of one another. When either his father or mother was alone with the children, he or she would be as loving and as warm as one would have wished one's parents to be. But as soon as the other appeared, the love and warmth vanished immediately; a sense of being caught red-handed would overcome the one who had been expressing feelings.

"It is not only that they do not have love for one another, but also that neither of them is permitted to show that he or she is capable of loving, or showing love to anybody else, not even to their own children," George said in an unmistakably and profoundly sad tone of voice.

It was the first time that I had heard him talking in such a tone. I had known him for several years, and not once had I heard him using any voice that revealed deep emotions. I felt guilty and thought that I was responsible, that somehow I had compelled him to reveal a part of his personal life that brought upon him an unfamiliar sense of sorrow. I felt guilty and wished that we could change the subject, or even reverse the conversation and go back to the moment when we were silent, or when he was going on about the "non-being of Being" or "Being-in-the-world" or anything else that allowed him to be as comfortably reserved as he used to be.

It was too late. I knew it was too late and could not help feeling guilty. And I started thinking of a way of making it up to him. I thought of Amina.

I thought that I should tell George about her, of what had happened to her, and how she was pushed to her own death. I thought I must reveal to him a dark secret of my own. I had never regarded what happened to Amina as a dark secret, or even a secret at all. I always felt that I would be willing to tell anybody who really wanted to know how Amina had actually died. And now, after having heard George's exceptional revelation, I thought I must reveal something of my own so that he and I could become even – so that neither of us, I thought, would perhaps feel stronger or weaker than the other.

Yes, I wanted to make it up to him one way or another, but somehow I realised that George would not like it. I thought if I told him the story of my sister's death, especially at that very moment, he would realise that I was trying to compensate for his revelation and he would then feel even more vulnerable. I had to make it up to him, I said to myself, and thought of Amina again. I imagined her running away with him. I pictured her as the new Palestinian woman which she was groomed to be, some-one who did exactly as she wished.

I thought of her living with George as husband and wife, not as runaways in America or Germany – something I had imagined before – but here in Lebanon, in our very area, defying everybody and living together. I thought of them making history, a Moslem woman marrying a Christian. Surely there could be nothing more daring for a society excessively concerned about who fucked whom, I said to myself.

A Moslem woman marrying a Christian, relatives, neighbours and friends would say with a grave sense of indignity. What next? they would ask, I thought, and felt satisfied. I felt happy for George and Amina first, and then satisfied for myself. Yet deep down I was sure that this fantasy was only meant to make me feel better. I felt guilty that I had pushed George to divulge what he would otherwise have preferred to keep to himself, and that fantasy about him and Amina was meant to redeem me of the sense of guilt.

It nearly succeeded but the problem was that George didn't want to stop talking about his parents. He went on revealing more of their secrets.

"You see," he continued, "they have been living together for the last twenty-seven years but most of it without being married," he said while looking at me, and when he realised that I was startled, as he expected me to be, he added: "they are divorced, they have been divorced for the last twenty years."

And he went on to explain how for all these years they managed to stay together, to live under the same roof, albeit in separate bedrooms, and deal with one another as no more than a pair of strangers. "A few relatives and friends have always known that they are divorced,"

George said. "As for us, the children, we were kept in the dark until we were in our twenties. Up till the time we were told, I had thought that this lack of intimacy between them was the norm for married couples. The limited social life that we all lived merely confirmed such a belief."

At this point I wanted to interrupt him, to ask questions, to get more details, or to say anything which would prove to him that I was listening not out of curiosity, but out of concern and care. I was feeling even more embarrassed and guilty, and I didn't know either how to stop him talking or how to turn his confession into a serious discussion between two responsible friends. But what he was saying sounded too personal to be anything other than a painful confession. At best it seemed like an attempt to get things off his chest. George wanted to talk, I thought, and it was too late for him to stop.

And he talked. He went on explaining how the lack of intimacy between his parents came to be, in his mind, the norm between married couples. That was how married people behaved towards one another, he believed. As for books and films, which claimed that things were different, he thought that they spread an altogether fake image of relationships between men and women, especially married ones. How all those floods of feelings and emotions that were displayed in films or talked about in books and magazines were contrary not only to what he had thought customary but were contrary to what was natural too. The long shared life of a couple, any couple, he came to accept, could not accommodate the shaky ground of

59

emotions and desires. Emotions were meant for Art alone, he said. Emotions, just like artistic visions, he said, were short-lived, and therefore they both went nicely together. And perhaps, I thought, that was why George never tried to discover the reason behind his parents' divorce or their remaining together for so many years afterwards. He didn't even try to ask questions. Of course, he would not have expected a straight answer even if he had. But he didn't ask anyway because he gradually came to believe that his parents, regardless of their own reasons, had done the right thing. Getting divorced after no more than seven years of marriage, yet continuing to live together, meant to him that from the beginning they had responsibly decided to face up to the prospect of worn-out passions and faded sexual desires. Their cutting it short, he thought, was a brave thing to do – a "remarkable embodiment of confronting the abyss of non-being," as he put it.

"Perhaps they didn't see it that way," he said after a moment of deep reflection in which he seemed to be weighing his judgment carefully, "but, by God, it's the achievement of their life."

I was surprised that he came to such a conclusion. I had expected him to show grave regret that his parents lived without love, or at least without showing emotions. I thought that he would use the lack of intimacy as an explanation for his detachment and fear of personal relationships. For a moment I thought of interrupting him and of disputing his claim, of telling him that his conclusion was an utter nonsense, but I was more disturbed by the way he was talking. He no longer spoke in a voice fraught with sadness, but more like someone who no longer cared, someone who wanted to embarrass himself and his listener at the same time. He sounded as if he actually wanted to tell me: "If that's what you have always been eager to know, then there they are, all the facts, laid out bare in front of you! I hope you are satisfied now!"

George didn't say what he was saying to me because he wanted to get things off his chest, I said to myself, nor because he wanted to confide in me as someone whom he could at last consider a close friend. It was obvious that he didn't. For, at that moment, he was not talking specifically to me, he was just talking. He looked as if he no longer had any sense of reserve and was willing to say what he was saying to whomever he judged to be curious about his life, and the life of his family. He was willing to talk in order to get rid of inquisitive people, I came to realise that evening. And for him, I thought, I must have been too curious a person, and perhaps an intruder. The way he spoke made me feel that I had pried into his life; that if he had decided to tell me what otherwise he would've preferred to keep to himself, it was because he wanted to get rid of me.

And perhaps, I thought to myself years later when I met Ali at Heathrow Airport, that was the real reason why I never revealed what George had told me. I must have felt guilty from the beginning, and decided to pretend that I had never heard it. Even after so many years, when I met Ali, I could not talk about it. Ali was eager to learn what I knew but I managed to avoid letting on what George had said that night.

George told me everything that night, and at the same time decided that he no longer wanted to have anything to do with me. I knew it right away. Then I realised that all the time he was talking, he was actually guiding me back home. It was he, not me, I realised, who was leading the way. He was the one who was so angry that he wanted to get rid of me at the earliest opportunity. He took me to my home, and the moment we reached the entrance to the building where I lived, he fell silent. It was not the kind of silence which meant that it was goodbye for now, it was the silence which implied that from then on we were going to see very little of one another.

It was no surprise that when the next morning I was told of Maher's disappearance, and I went looking for him asking friends and acquaintances, I didn't go to George. For a moment I thought of going to tell him, but I remembered the night before and what he had told me and how it had all ended. I realised that I couldn't see him again, that the distance which had kept me, and all of us, from him was lost. And with its loss the sort of friendship that we had maintained – a friendship which was only possible as long as we kept away from each other's personal lives – had come to an end. George after all was that kind of friend whom one could lose very easily, I thought without any sense of loss or regret.

3

It was the night when the four of us were together for the last time. That night Maher realised that the past had caught up with him sooner than he had expected.

After Ali had left us, Maher too decided to go home, but he never got there. For as he turned into the street where he lived he saw an unfamiliar civilian car parked nearby. He immediately thought that Israeli Intelligence had come for him – the car looked just like the ones Israeli Intelligence used in their regular rounds. He was gripped by fear, but was also surprised. He didn't expect that the Israelis would ever suspect him of belonging to the Resistance. True, he often bragged about working for the Resistance, but he never suspected anyone would take it seriously enough to report him. It must have been Bassem who snitched on him, he thought – Bassem, the drug pusher who was murdered a few weeks earlier.

Yes! It must've been him who reported me to the Israelis before he was killed by the Resistance! he said to himself. Then he cursed us, Ali and me, assuming that we were the ones who had blabbed in front of Bassem. He cursed us again and decided to make a run for it, but before he managed to turn back the car doors were flung open and three men jumped out and strode towards him. He realised that there was no point in trying to run away. On the contrary, he thought, running away would just make things worse. So he decided to stay and talk to them, hoping that he would be able to persuade them that they were after the wrong person.

He was still frightened and surprised, and all the more so when he heard them talking Arabic, not Hebrew. They were Lebanese; he could tell from their accent. Collaborators, no doubt, he thought, and realised that things were worse than he had anticipated. With the Israelis, you knew who you were dealing with and why you were being arrested. What was more important you knew what was awaiting you: a few days of interrogation and then a transfer to Ansar prison. But with these buggers, you didn't know why you were being arrested nor what would happen to you. He hastened to tell them that they must have made a mistake. He was not given a chance to explain, however. Instead he was shouted and sworn at, and then dragged onto the back seat of the car.

"I've done nothing!" he protested in an imploring tone as the car sped away through the dark, deserted streets of the city under curfew. Nobody would see him being dragged away. Nor would anyone hear him begging for mercy.

He was shouted at and told to shut up, but Maher couldn't help repeating his full name and claiming that he was absolutely innocent, and insisting that they must have made a mistake. And he didn't stop until the driver eventually got fed up with him.

"And what about ruining people's lives? Is that innocent too?" the driver demanded, looking at him in the rear view mirror. Maher didn't know what the driver was talking about. He was too frightened to remember or even to think straight. He just went on begging and repeating that he had done nothing.

"No? Nothing at all?" the irritated driver asked, with one eye on the road ahead and the other on the rear view mirror.

"No! Never!" Maher replied.

"Never? But what about Abu Hanna, what about ruining his life?" shouted the driver. He was so angry that he could no longer drive. He stopped the car with such a sudden jolt that it startled the three passengers. They could not avoid falling forwards, and Maher's head hit the back of the front seat violently. Overwhelmed with rage, the driver didn't seem to have noticed what had happened. He got out and started pacing up and down the side of the road.

The passenger in the front seat got out too. He was very worried. He looked around hoping nobody would see them; then he walked around the car to where the driver was angrily pacing up and down, and tried to calm him down. He told the driver that they must continue before anybody appeared, because an Israeli patrol might come their way and think they belonged to the Resistance. And if that happened, the man warned, they were finished. The driver was too angry to listen. The fact that one of his companions was trying to calm him down must have made him feel ashamed that he had lost his temper so easily. Yet realising such a fact seemed to make him even angrier.

"Get out of the car, you son of a bitch!" he shouted at Maher, throwing open the back door next to Maher.

Maher didn't move. He was terrified at such an abrupt demand, and hoped that the other man would intervene and prevent the driver from doing what he suddenly intended to do.

"Get out!" shouted the driver again. Glaring at the man in the back seat guarding Maher, he yelled at him: "Push him out now!"

The man started shoving Maher while the one standing by the driver tried to intervene, hoping to change his mind. He told him that they should not do anything right there. He reminded him again of the risk of confronting an Israeli patrol, but the driver insisted on getting him out.

"I want him now!" the driver shouted, "right now, I tell you!"

"Wait until we are far enough away from here!" the man went on, begging in a low voice.

But the driver didn't want to listen and, taking out his pistol, he grabbed Maher by his shirt collar and dragged him towards the far side of the road. He aimed the pistol at Maher's head and as he was about to pull the trigger he heard Maher begging for mercy and pleading that he wasn't the one responsible for his father's ruin.

Yes, the driver was Hanna, the son of Abu Hanna. He was surprised that Maher had recognised him. He did not expect Maher to know him. They had never met before, and for a few seconds he thought of asking him how he knew he was Abu Hanna's son. His anger was greater than his curiosity, and if his father's name earlier on had triggered his rage and made him incapable of driving, now that Maher himself mentioned his father, it made him even more uncontrollable.

Without any further hesitation he pulled the trigger,

turned and walked back to the car. His two companions looked at him in dismay. They hadn't expected this. They were frightened of him.

Recounting what had happened that night, one of the kidnappers who was captured and interrogated by the Resistance just after the Israeli withdrawal from the area, said that he had actually expected Hanna to ask one of them to take care of Maher. He didn't think that Hanna was capable of using a gun, he said, but it seemed that he wanted desperately to avenge his father's ruin and early death.

"After he shot Maher and walked back towards the car," the kidnapper said, "he looked relieved. He nodded at us as if to inform us that the job was at last done. And without any trace of his earlier rage, he asked us to get into the car, and we simply drove off without another word."

That's what the kidnapper said. He could have been lying. He probably wanted to lay the blame for Maher's murder wholly on Hanna's shoulders. He was also trying to show that there was a strong motive for Hanna to kill Maher. Maher had caused his father's ruin, and consequently his death. And even if this was not considered a good enough reason for Hanna's revenge, Hanna was, by then, safe from punishment. He had returned to France, where he had been living before his father's death.

"When Abu Hannah died," said the kidnapper under interrogation, "Hanna had to come back. He knew what had happened, he realised that his father had died heartbroken, and he swore revenge."

After a moment's silence, he added in a somewhat regretful tone that Hanna was not actually sure whether he had shot the right person. "All the way back," the kidnapper said, "Hanna kept repeating: 'The bastard said that he was not responsible for my father's ruin'. Of course Hanna couldn't be sure, nor could the two of us who had helped him kidnap Maher!"

Years later when I met Ali at Heathrow Airport we talked about Maher's tragic fate and agreed that he was not responsible for what had happened to Abu Hanna. In all honesty nobody could have claimed that he was responsible, I said, and Ali nodded in agreement. He might have caused some of the mess that took place, but he certainly didn't mean it to end the way it did.

Ali agreed but he didn't seem keen to hear more about it. The memory of that time, from the night when Maher disappeared until the discovery of his body two days later, was doubly painful for Ali. It was then that his brother Sameh was arrested by the Resistance and all the subsequent troubles that enveloped Ali and his family started. Sameh himself was killed a few weeks later; Ali and his father were arrested by the Israelis, and soon after Ali was compelled to become an Israeli informer.

During our meeting at Heathrow I couldn't help noticing how gloomy and distracted Ali looked the moment I started talking about the events of Maher's kidnapping and murder. I began to recall that morning when Maher's brothers came to see me. "Maher didn't come home last night," they told me, and they were extremely worried. They had hoped that he had stayed with me. I told them that he hadn't, and suggested that he might be with Ali.

It was not unusual for him to stay at Ali's place. Ali was closer to him than either George or me. Besides, Ali's parents were more hospitable than George's or mine. Whenever Maher stayed out late, or had a fight with his parents, he would stay at Ali's. I was actually a bit surprised that Maher's brothers didn't go to see Ali first, and I nearly said so, but they looked upset and worried enough. I myself started to feel worried, remembering the Israeli patrol which George and I had miraculously missed the night before. For a second, I thought Maher had perhaps not been as lucky as us. Suddenly agitated, I decided to go with them to see Ali.

When we met him, surprisingly enough, he looked anxious and distracted too. For one moment I thought that he must have already known about Maher's disappearance. But soon I realised that his obvious worry and distraction had nothing to do with Maher. He didn't know about his friend's fate until I told him.

"Maher didn't go home last night," I said pointing to Maher's two brothers who were increasingly nervous.

"Maher as well?" he said vaguely, and looked astonished and helpless.

I didn't understand what he meant, nor could I ask him if anybody else had disappeared as well. The moment I realised that Maher hadn't stayed with him, I assumed that he must have been picked up by the Israeli patrol. And it seemed that I wasn't the only one who was almost certain that Maher was either arrested by the Israelis or kidnapped by their collaborators. Maher's two brothers were in total panic and Ali looked hopelessly confused and disheartened. In spite of my worry, though, I could not help being a bit curious. I didn't expect Ali to react this way. I had thought that if anybody could keep a clear head in such circumstances, it would be him. Actually when I suggested to Maher's brothers that we should go to Ali's home, it was not so much because I was sure that Maher would be there but rather because I was certain that Ali would be able to deal with the situation better than either Maher's brothers or me. Up till then I had not known that Ali himself had his own troubles. I was surprised that he had looked so worried, I remembered when I was sitting with him at Heathrow Airport. Yet as soon as he asked "Maher as well?" it was obvious that something else was wrong. I assumed that it had to do with Sameh, but I didn't know for sure until two weeks later after Sameh was shot dead, and Ali and his father were arrested and detained at Israeli HQ.

When, seventeen years later, I met Ali at Heathrow Airport and talked to him about the circumstances of Maher's murder, he looked as distracted as he had that morning when Maher's brothers and I went to see him. The circumstances of Maher's disappearance took place at exactly the same time as those disastrous events which had changed Ali's own life for good. I felt embarrassed and wished that I had not mentioned that particular time. I immediately hoped that by remaining silent I would give him the chance of recalling something he would rather talk about. Ali didn't want to change the subject, however. He must have realised how awkward his reaction had made me, and thought there was no reason why we shouldn't discuss everything that had taken place then.

Resuming our recollection of what had happened to Maher, he said that Maher wasn't responsible for the destruction of Abu Hanna's factory: "It was Salim who blew it up!" he said in a surprisingly casual voice and then looked at me, as if he was drawing my attention to an important fact that should have been obvious to me.

"Yes, I know," I said, "but that was what Abu Hanna, and his son, and some other people, believed. They assumed that Maher was the one who put him up to it."

It was indeed Salim who had blown up the factory. We all knew that. Some time before the explosion, Maher had stopped going to the factory or meeting Salim, yet people couldn't help feeling that somehow Maher had a hand in it. Some even thought that he was totally responsible. After all, it was he who had filled Salim's head with all that nonsense about the workers being exploited by factory owners. That's what Abu Hanna said the morning he turned up at the factory and found it reduced to a heap of rubble.

"He put him up to this," he said, stretching his arm towards the ruined factory, "Salim would've never done it by himself."

People who heard him thought that he was blaming

Maher in person, and he probably was. But I thought, as did Ali, that what Abu Hanna meant to say was that it was not only an idiot like Salim, but all those who were behind him. Of course that meant Maher, but also all those political parties and militias who thought and talked like him.

"All the bastards in Lebanon!" he cried out as he looked at the people who had gathered there immediately after they had heard that explosion. "All the bastards!" he said as he packed up what was left of his business and left. He returned to his village devastated by what had been done to him; the end of a long-established family business and the ruin of his only source of income.

A few months later he died. Grief killed him, we were told. Just before he died he would walk the roads of his village, talking to himself, we were told. When his son, Hanna, learned about his father's death he came back to Lebanon swearing to take revenge. He promised to kill the person responsible, even if it took him ten or twenty years. Realising that he couldn't take his revenge there and then, he reasoned that he might have to wait before the situation in Lebanon, or at least in our area, had changed. But, as it turned out, he didn't have to wait long. A few months after the start of the Israeli invasion he was able to get into a car accompanied by two of his friends, and drive into the city looking for the man whom he believed was responsible for his father's ruin and death.

As a result of the Israeli invasion of 1982, armed men from Abu Hanna's village, among other local armed groups, had taken over our arena. A small militia of collaborators, they could go into most areas which had fallen under Israeli occupation and do whatever they wanted. Hanna himself did not belong to such a militia, but some of his friends and relatives did, and it was with the help of two such friends that he managed to kidnap Maher and kill him.

Hanna was never sure whether he should get Maher or Salim, or both, for what had happened to his father. He knew that it was Salim who actually blew up the factory. He also knew that although Maher had persuaded Salim that he and the rest of the workers in the factory were being exploited, Maher had never actually encouraged Salim to do harmful things. Later, the kidnapper who was interrogated by the Resistance said that Hanna could not help accepting his father's judgment, or what he thought was his father's judgment, that Maher was behind the whole thing, and that Salim was a mere puppet in Maher's hands.

"Hanna wanted to convince himself that Maher was the guilty person, and the only guilty person," the kidnapper said. "For that reason he started making things up. He claimed that Maher was extorting money from his father, and that when his father refused to pay up, he incited Salim to blow up the factory."

Hanna didn't think that Salim was entirely blameless, said the kidnapper. He certainly would have wished to make him pay as well, but Salim was not easy to get at. He was living in the Camp, and the Camp, like most Palestinian refugee camps, was under tighter Israeli control than the city. Any arrest that was to take place there had to be authorised by the Israelis themselves, and Hanna's two companions were not influential enough to get such authorisation.

Yes, it was Comrade Salim, I said to myself and remembered how pleased Maher was of Salim, or Comrade Salim, as he used to call him. "Comrade Salim said this today," he would proudly announce to us, "isn't that amazing?" Or "Today I explained to Comrade Salim the theory of surplus value," he once said, "and guess what, he got it the first time round, and in a way it was as if he had always known it but was never able to express it in his own words!"

He was so proud of Salim, and would explain to us what he called the "objective conditions" which had made Salim socially radical. "His revolutionary potential is not the outcome of reading and studying theory, but of experience and practical social consciousness," he said in a loud and confident voice.

We were sitting in Ramadan Café, but Maher had nothing to worry about. He knew that Hajj Ramadan wasn't there and so felt free to boast about Salim in whatever way he felt, without fear of the owner shouting "No politics, please!" But I had the feeling that George would have preferred it if Hajj Ramadan had been there. He looked bored and sometimes pretended that he wasn't listening. Ali and I, on the other hand, kept smiling and nodding. That was the only thing we could do to prove to Maher that we were paying attention to what he was saying. We had taken drugs and it was very hard for us to concentrate on what was being said. Maher guessed that we had taken something, but he was too excited about Salim's "revolutionary potential" to lecture us, as he often did, about the danger of drugs and wasting our energy in that way. He knew that he was practically talking to himself, but he didn't seem to mind. He was so proud of his discovery of Salim.

Years later, after I had come to London and was considering writing my PhD on the experiences of my generation, I remembered how much Maher was taken by Salim, and I realised exactly what Maher's fault was: he was too excited to see the social difference between himself and Salim, and to know that such a profound difference was bound to lead to trouble. He did not take into account the fact that, unlike him, Salim was working in the factory because he could hardly do anything else. Salim didn't have any qualifications or skills to practise a decent profession. He had left school before completing his primary education and had never gone into any professional training. He was still living with his family in the Camp. In other words he was still a refugee in a social and economic sense as much as in a political and legal sense.

What Maher had failed to foresee, was that Salim, unlike Maher himself, was not the sort of person who sought a dogma that he could preach. He didn't seek some belief just to win arguments. Instead he wanted a dogma that could help him change the precarious situation into which he was born and in which he had grown up, at least to give him some hope that such a situation could one day be changed.

By contrast Maher was happy enough just to preach his dogma and win arguments in its name. That's why he would invariably stop harassing Abu Hanna when eventually he won the argument.

Salim, on the other hand, I thought, could not stop at that and felt that he must go further than winning an argument, so he blew up the factory. Of course he didn't blow up the factory because he thought that by doing so he was changing things, but because ultimately he felt betrayed. He wanted to assert that, unlike Maher, his taking up a dogma was not merely an intellectual exercise. And if it was ever an exercise, it was the exercise of his own life.

Maher didn't understand this attitude. In fact, none of us did until years later, and when we, at least Ali and I, managed to look at our situation from a distance, we came to realise what we never had enough courage to acknowledge at the time: namely, that though we were still refugees in the legal and political sense, economically and socially speaking we had become more of a middle class, albeit a funny kind of middle class.

When I thought of it this way, I could not help feeling embarrassed. It was the first time that I had considered my family and people like my family as middle class, or at least labelled them as such. To be honest I had expected to be more surprised than embarrassed, but I was not surprised. The directness of such a description, I said to myself, did away with the expected surprise. It acknowledged the shame and was vulgar enough to make my sense of embarrassment greater.

Then, I thought, we must have all been deeply aware of the fact that the relative prosperity we had enjoyed was the outcome of moving from the refugee camp to the city, and then merging into the local middle class. We must have regarded such prosperity as somehow a betrayal of our origins, and we probably felt guilty about that. The acknowledgment of such shame made the description "middle class" infer nothing but snobbishness. Maher must have realised this fact, or at least acknowledged it to himself, before any of us did. The excessive enthusiasm that he had shown for reading Marxist pamphlets was an attempt to prove that he was still faithful to his origins, and that he had not neglected what he often called the double duty, "our class duty and our national duty". Of course we often made fun of his double duty, but years later, when I came to see it differently, I realised that beneath that ill-chosen term "our double duty" was a profound sense of shame. I also realised that his frequent reference to what he called "class consciousness" expressed his constant awareness of the distance that separated our present lives in the city from our past life in the Camp. It was for that reason, I imagined, that Maher didn't only read Marxist pamphlets but also tried to see our very lives through them. Such pamphlets must have helped him to rationalise the life in the Camp and in the city, the past and the present of people like us, as a part of one social structure with different classes. He often referred to the people of the Camp as "working class", as if he was trying to reduce the distance which separated them from people like us into a social distance – a distance that separated one class from another. It was for this very reason, I believed, that when he eventually decided to act upon what he had learned from those pamphlets, he made sure to contact Palestinian workers from the Camp. And that was probably also why he sought out those whose parents or grandparents came from the same village in Palestine as his own parents: Maher's parents came from Tarshiha, and so did Salim's.

I decided to write on this very subject: about those of us who had moved from the Camp to the city, and on the way that they perceived both themselves and those whom they had left behind. It was Maher's story which had actually encouraged me to think that our life was a suitable topic for academic study – it made me look at our life as an area waiting to be discovered and I decided to make this journey of discovery. My PhD, I thought, would be something totally new.

However, I was more tempted to tell the story of Maher than to embark upon writing a scholarly dissertation. Maher's story was a farce that ended in tragedy. He had read those red-covered Marxist pamphlets, which the Soviet Cultural Centre in Beirut distributed in those days. After reading them he started contacting members of the Communist Party and for a while they saw him as a potential recruit and invited him to some of their meetings. At first he was very excited and kept talking about this experience as if it was the greatest thing that had ever happened in his life. Soon, however, his excitement faded away and he stopped seeing them. It turned out, as he confessed to us, that only a very few members of the Party that he knew actually read the pamphlets that he had read. Whenever he tried to have a decent political discussion with his comrades, he told us – that is George, Ali and me, who were trying very hard to keep a straight face – he felt that most of them lacked knowledge of the basic precepts of Marxism. In fact, he added, he soon learnt that they were actually not so very different from the vulgar members of the other political parties and militias. Disappointed, Maher decided not to become a Party member. Instead he chose to remain an independent Marxist and act on his own.

"I shall get in touch directly with members of the radical class!" he declared, and looked at us hoping that we would ask him to tell us more about his new plan.

"What radical class?" I asked, more out of annoyance than the desire to know. By then we had heard enough of his political adventures and none of us had the slightest desire to hear more.

"What radical class?" he replied. "Don't you know what radical class? The working class, of course, the people who have gained their class consciousness the hard way and consequently have appreciated the revolutionary role . . . "

"Yes, but there is no working class in this area!" I interrupted him impatiently, and looked at both George and Ali to encourage them to say something to support me. But neither uttered a word. The only thing I got back was a sullen look from Ali, as if to tell me, "Can't you shut your mouth and stop giving him excuses to keep talking about his shit radical class!" It was too late, though, and we had to listen to him giving a long and windy reply to my objection.

A few days later Maher started paying regular visits to Abu Hanna's factory. It was one of those small old factories that by sheer luck had managed to survive both progress and war. It specialised in making traditional sweets and employed no more than a dozen or so workers. The factory was one of these old places that didn't bother to have a guard at its gate, apart from its owner, Abu Hanna, who was a tolerant man. Being a Christian Lebanese in an area dominated largely by Moslems, Lebanese and Palestinians, Abu Hanna could not afford to have enemies in the neighbourhood, especially enemies from those who belonged to political parties and militias. On the contrary he was particularly keen to be friendly towards both members and leaders of those parties and militias. When Maher started frequenting his factory, Abu Hanna was wary but made no attempt to stop him. After all, Maher came to the factory during the lunch break and none of the workers, at least at the beginning, was neglecting his duty as a result of his visit. Even when Abu Hanna realised that some of the workers, particularly Salim, who had grown close to Maher, started to extend their lunch break, he did nothing. He hoped that soon enough one of them would get bored of the other.

Abu Hanna didn't want any trouble and tried to overcome this problem of Maher's visits, especially when they became more regular and longer than he could tolerate, by befriending Maher himself. On more than one occasion he would invite him into his little office, make him coffee and give him two or three slabs of halawa as a gift. He assured him that he did not mind seeing an educated man like him coming to the factory and talking to the workers. In fact, he said, the workers probably needed an educated man who could advise them on various matters, particularly those of social and moral concern.

Maher enjoyed receiving the gifts and the flattery. He particularly enjoyed being called an educated man, precisely because he had never been good at school and his parents thought it would have been better for him to take up some useful craft or to join his eldest sister and her husband in America. However, he would have preferred to be called an intellectual, a revolutionary intellectual of course; but being called an educated man was a good start.

Still he could not help being suspicious that the gift of halawa and the flattery were a mere bribe. He feared that Abu Hanna wished to bribe him so that he would give up on what he had set out to achieve; that is, to open the eyes of the workers of the factory to the fact that they were victims of capitalist exploitation. As Maher once told us, after he had just come back from the factory, he knew that trying to buy revolutionary intellectuals was something which capitalists could never resist. Jokingly, George asked him whether he intended to return the halawa to Abu Hanna as a way of informing him that he was not the sort of revolutionary intellectual who could be bought, and certainly not by two slabs of halawa. We all laughed but Maher didn't. In a rather embarrassed tone of voice he told us that the halawa had already been eaten; but he assured us that he was willing to pay for it the moment he realised that Abu Hanna expected him to give up his mission.

"I shall make it clear to him," he said to us, "that nothing will stop me from explaining to every worker that he is being exploited."

And he actually did. Every time he went to the factory and talked to a worker, or at least the three or four who cared to listen to him, he told them how they were being exploited. Using the Marxist jargon that he had learned, he went on explaining how it all worked out in favour of the owner of the factory, and that they, the workers, ended up putting in more than they took out, and deserved to take out. Expressions such as "the means of production" and "relations of production" were particularly helpful in making his case.

Abu Hanna himself was surprised when he heard Maher making such claims. He had often heard of bosses who exploited their workers, but he had never thought he was considered one of them. Abu Hanna tried to assure Maher that no exploitation of any kind was taking place. He was an honest man, he told him, and he always paid his workers their rights in full. Furthermore, since the factory was established some fifty years earlier, no worker had ever left feeling that he had been cheated. If anything, both he and his father and grandfather, who managed the factory before him, were always proud of being fair to those who worked for them. It was more of a tradition, he said, to treat workers as members of the family, to take interest in their private affairs and help them in difficult times.

Maher was amused to see Abu Hanna so taken back by the accusation of exploiting his workers, and naturally eager to defend himself and the factory's proud record. For a moment he thought of telling Abu Hanna that he knew that he, Abu Hanna, was an honest boss who did not cheat his workers. Nor, for that matter, did he consider him to be someone who exploited them in the common meaning of the term. Instead, he explained to Abu Hanna that the exploitation he was talking about was more of an "objective" sort, an exploitation that was inherent in the capitalist system within which the factory operated. He thought of explaining the situation in this way so that Abu Hanna could feel at ease. But then he believed it was better to leave him feeling awkward and on the defensive. It would be easier for him to accuse Abu Hanna of maintaining that system of exploitation, even though he was not responsible for its existence or indeed aware of it.

"It was very hard to explain such a thing to a man like Abu Hanna," Maher told us after he had been to see him, "a man who doesn't know the ABC of Marxist economy."

None of us said anything. We were bored but, as usual, that didn't prevent him from going on, reporting with great enthusiasm the outcome of his meeting: "For example," he said, "Abu Hanna didn't seem to know what 'surplus value' was. And if he had managed to assume that the 'means of production' are the factory and its old machinery he was totally mystified as to the implication of 'relations of production'. However, when I explained it to him he was relieved to realise that the exploitation of which he was accused was actually the outcome of 'the relations of production'."

Thus, Maher explained, Abu Hanna was able to claim that he personally was neither responsible for the inherent exploitation nor was he able to put an end to it. It was, he told Maher – who was amazed to see Abu Hanna so forthcoming in responding to the argument and also in using Marxist expressions – a system which went beyond the limits of his own factory and all the other small factories in Lebanon.

Maher had to acknowledge that the man was right. He was actually glad to do so. Abu Hanna had unequivocally admitted that he was exploiting his workers, and what was more important, at least for Maher, that by making such an admission he actually, albeit unknowingly, endorsed Marxist theory. As for the fact that Abu Hanna had evaded all responsibility for such exploitation, Maher thought that was beside the point. He dismissed the fact, which Ali and I pointed out several times in our discussions with him, that Abu Hanna clearly showed no intention of putting an end to such exploitation. According to Marxist theory, Maher continued, it was not the business of the owner of a factory to put an end to the state of exploitation. This, he added with some irritation that we didn't get this very simple point ourselves, was the historical role of the working class. Besides, he went on rhetorically, what difference would it make if Abu Hanna had handed over the factory to the workers? None at all, he answered his own question. The state of exploitation was not going to end because one owner of a factory gave up his factory to his employees: "The workers all over the country," he exclaimed, hitting the table with his fist, "must seize the means of production and consequently change the relations of production!"

Years later, when I remembered Maher and thought of writing my dissertation on the gap between the social and the political states of our lives back in the Lebanon, I realised that ending the state of exploitation, which he kept ranting about, was not his main concern after all. I knew that when Maher started to frequent the factory he was not thinking of any practical way to stop the exploitation of the workers, he just wanted to examine in the real world the thoughts and claims which he had learned from those little red-covered Marxist pamphlets. He desperately wanted an assurance that such ideas and claims were correct, and it was for that reason, I said to myself, that he, ironically enough, grew to like Abu Hanna. Abu Hanna had told him exactly what he wanted to hear, and he felt satisfied. He actually felt so satisfied that he stopped going to see the workers, and instead started to see Abu Hanna.

The factory workers, or at least those who had bothered to listen to him, especially Salim, were baffled with such a reversal of attitude. Maher was supposed to come to see them, they thought – and especially Salim. He was supposed to be on their side. They felt let down by him. Salim in particular felt betrayed, and as a result, he started making trouble. First he started quarrelling with other workers, and then he started rowing with Abu Hanna and neglecting his work. He accused Abu Hanna of exploiting him and the other workers, and began making unreasonable demands. Every other day he would come to Abu Hanna's office and ask for a pay rise, or for fewer hours of work, or make other demands which no other factory was giving to its workers. Nor could Abu Hanna afford it. Abu Hanna tried to reason with him, but to no avail. In the end he had no other option but to fire him.

Salim was fired and Maher stopped visiting the factory. He felt too embarrassed to return and meet Abu Hanna and the other workers after what had happened to Salim. He felt responsible for the change in Salim's attitude and behaviour and thought it best to keep away from the factory.

But that was not the only reason why he stopped going to the factory. He had nothing more to do, and no one to talk to. After he had switched his interest from the workers to Abu Hanna he had very little to say or do in the factory. Abu Hanna had agreed with whatever he said, so after a few meetings they had run out of things to say.

Maher had to stop going to the factory. And had it not been for Salim, or more precisely for what Salim had done, Maher would have probably forgotten all about it. He would have considered the whole affair as just one episode in his "revolutionary life", as he used to put it. But a few weeks after he had stopped going to the factory, Salim blew it up. Salim demolished the factory, and Maher was blamed. For months he couldn't bear to hear anything about the factory, or Salim or Abu Hanna, without feeling totally embarrassed.

*

But that night, the last night when the four of us were together, and when I jokingly referred to "Comrade Salim", we all thought that we were talking about something that had been forgotten. Of course we were wrong; that very evening Maher was kidnapped and killed and two days later his body was found on the eastern route out of the city. "His eyes were wide open!" I heard one of the people who found him say. I tried to imagine Maher in those terrifying last moments of his life, looking in disbelief at his assassin.

"It was one bullet to the head," I heard that person repeating, and again I tried to imagine what Maher must have felt before the trigger was pulled. Soon, however, I found myself thinking of Amina. The words "one bullet to the head" made me remember Amina, made me remember that afternoon, ten years earlier, when I heard a shot in the next room. We, mother, my brother Kamal and I, forced our way in and found Amina lying on the floor in a pool of blood. It was one bullet to the head. "Amina's pulled the trigger," I remembered saying in horror, "Amina's pulled the trigger."

It was something that I wanted my brother Kamal to hear. It was an answer to Kamal's question: "But can you pull the trigger, Amina, can you pull it?" I remembered Kamal asking her, teasing her the day she had come home carrying a pistol: "Can you pull the trigger, Comrade Amina? Can you?" he asked teasingly. "Do you have the courage to pull the trigger, Comrade Amina?"

That day Maher's body was found I remembered it all. I

remembered it all, but I also realised that Kamal was not only teasing her. The bully was testing her. He wanted to know whether she was prepared to use the gun to defend herself. He wanted to go on bullying her without the fear of her using the gun against him. The bully was frightened of her, I thought that day when Maher's body was found. And in spite of the grief that had overwhelmed me, I could not help feeling some sense of satisfaction.

4

It was the last night when the four of us were together.

That night three men in their twenties came to see Abu Ali, Ali's father. They introduced themselves as being "from the Resistance", and without preamble told him that they were detaining his son.

At first Abu Ali thought that they had come to talk to him about Ali. He had always suspected that sooner or later Ali was going to get himself into trouble. The company that he kept was bound to upset one group or another in the area: the Israelis and their collaborators from the local militias, on the one hand; or, on the other hand, the Resistance and those who pretended that they were from the Resistance. Waiting to learn exactly what Ali had done, Abu Ali couldn't help wondering whether these three men were actually from the Resistance or were merely pretending. There were a lot of people who pretended to belong to the Resistance. He grew more suspicious when he noticed that only one of them was talking while the other two kept totally silent all through the meeting. He wondered whether it would have been safer for them if they had sent one person only, the one who took it upon himself to explain the aim of their visit. And if so, they would have saved themselves the risk of revealing the identity of two more of their men, especially as these two men neither did nor said anything.

At one stage, Abu Ali could not help imagining that at any moment the two men would start chuckling, and then the third one would burst out laughing, telling him that they had nothing to do with the Resistance and that they were only trying to play a little joke on him. He hoped that that would happen and he promised himself not to feel offended or angry. He expected them to start laughing, but instead he was told that the disgraceful behaviour of his son was the cause of his arrest. He realised that they were serious, and most surprisingly, that they were not talking about Ali but about his second son, Sameh.

Abu Ali had never thought that Sameh could be harmful or annoying to any political group, least of all to the Resistance. Of course he was well aware of the shameful weakness of his younger son. In fact, he felt endlessly disgusted by Sameh's behaviour – so much so that on more than one occasion he had thought of poisoning him. Nevertheless he had never believed that such a matter would be of any interest to the Resistance. He nearly asked them why the Resistance should worry itself with the personal behaviour of his son, even if it were disgusting, when it had a military occupation to fight. But their decisively authoritative manner made him refrain from so doing. It seemed to him that they believed that upholding moral conduct was an unquestionable duty of theirs, and he didn't want to sound as if he disagreed with them. He was aware of the fact that only a few weeks earlier they had shot a man for being a drug pusher.

Abu Ali could not question their authority; nobody could, or even seemed to want to. On the contrary, people cheered them for keeping up moral standards. But, then again, people were in the habit of cheering whoever had the upper hand. When Palestinian factions and left-wing parties were dominant, Abu Ali remembered, people joined them and cheered them, and when the Israelis came they applauded them and thanked them for getting rid of the Palestinians, now they were cheering the Resistance.

Abu Ali himself was a hypocrite, and as soon as he managed to grasp what had been said by that young man he went on to express his full approval of what the men of the Resistance had done.

"Yes," he said in an imploring way, "I wish you could teach him a lesson! To make a man out of that rotten sod!"

"That's exactly what we hope to do."

Abu Ali was relieved. For a moment he had feared that they were going to kill him. They were already killing drug pushers and they were more than willing to kill deviants like his son. But had they wanted to kill him, they would not have bothered to come and tell him first. He soon realised that the aim of their visit was not actually to inform him of his son's arrest, but to lay their hands on the van which Abu Ali used for his business.

The young man who spoke all the time told him that they wanted to smuggle weapons for their comrades in the south, and thought it would have been a good idea to borrow Abu Ali's van, especially as Sameh had already agreed to do the driving. Somehow everything fitted together very well. The young man said Sameh was willing to work for them, and the Resistance needed both a van and a driver. To assign the driving to Sameh would certainly make it easier to pass through Israeli check points, said the young man. After all, he would only be driving his father's van!

Abu Ali didn't know what to say. He had agreed that his son should be punished, but he didn't want him to get involved with the Resistance. Nor did he wish to allow his van to be used for smuggling weapons. He also knew that he could not refuse their request, nor could he try persuading them not to use his son as a driver. He knew that he had to look and sound as if he were in full agreement with them, otherwise they might get angry and decide to shoot Sameh for no reason other than that he had hesitated in agreeing with them. At that moment he wished only that Ali was there. He did not often wish to have him around, especially when he was dealing with customers; but now he could have been useful to say what he, Abu Ali, didn't dare say.

Ali could have risked testing how serious these men were, or how determined. Ali could have refused to give up his van and demand the immediate release of his brother. However, if it turned out that these men were not bluffing, and were determined to get their way, he, Abu Ali, could always have interfered, rebuffed Ali and promised them that everything would be done exactly as they wanted. This was the kind of trick which he played with some of his difficult clients.

Abu Ali decided to send for Ali. He went to the living room, where the rest of the family was waiting anxiously, and asked his youngest son to go to the café to fetch Ali. Om Ali wanted to know what the three men wanted. She looked both worried and confused. Like her husband, she had thought that something had happened to Ali; but when Abu Ali came into the room and told his youngest son to fetch Ali, she realised that the men were there for something, or someone else.

"What do they want?" she asked Abu Ali, getting more worried, but he had no time to explain things to her. He was more concerned to get Ali home as soon as possible.

But Ali arrived too late to play the role his father had wished for him. He was too late even to catch a glimpse of the three men of the Resistance. So Abu Ali had no option but to hand over the keys to the van. He walked out with them to where it was parked. It was a new van, bought only a few months earlier, and the three men couldn't conceal their delight at getting hold of it. They actually looked so happy that Abu Ali could not help entertaining his earlier suspicions that they didn't actually belong to the Resistance but were swindlers who went around conning people in the name of the Resistance. And for a moment he thought of asking for his keys back, only he didn't have the courage. He stood there watching them so excited at his expense and couldn't say a word. He now wished that they would get in and drive off at once. They didn't move. They went round examining the van as if they had just bought it and wanted to make sure that they had got what they had paid for. And as if to add insult to injury, one of them came to ask him for the spare tyre.

Abu Ali thought of asking him "Don't you want the clothes I am wearing too?" but instead he silently pointed to a flat box at the back of the van. The man went back, opened the box and checked the tyre was there. A look of satisfaction lit up his face. There was also a box of tools, and he checked that too. Eventually he got in, sat behind the wheel and continued to examine and check every-thing. Another man sat beside him; the two of them talked for a few minutes and then drove away, leaving the third standing on the pavement opposite where Abu Ali was standing.

It was the same man who had done all the talking before. He waited until the van disappeared and the sound of the engine died away; then he crossed the street to Abu Ali. With an overconfident tone of voice, he told Abu Ali that the Resistance appreciated his handing over of the van and that everything would be done in order to ensure the safety of his son Sameh.

He must have noticed the look of unease on Abu Ali's face and wished to assure him that they were not swindlers, and that they genuinely belonged to the Resistance. But Abu Ali didn't feel any better; the sense of having been blackmailed into accepting the fate of his son and having given away his van took an even tighter hold on him. At that very moment, the last thing he wished to be assured of was that those men genuinely belonged to the Resistance. On the contrary, he thought, he would have preferred it if the whole thing were a hoax. At least his son would have been out of danger and he would have retained the hope of retrieving his van.

He wished that Ali had returned earlier but by the time he arrived they had taken the van and disappeared. Abu Ali was still suspicious, or at least retained the hope that the three young men were only swindlers. He urged Ali to get in touch with others in the Resistance to check whether they were genuine.

Abu Ali had always believed that Ali had friends in the Resistance. He didn't approve of such friendships – he never approved of any of Ali's friends – but now he didn't mind benefiting from them. Ali didn't know anybody in the Resistance though. There was Maher of course, Ali thought, but Maher, as we all knew, was one of those who went round boasting that they were busy doing "Resistance work". Ali did not believe that Maher really knew anybody in the Resistance nor did he know whom to ask, or where to ask, not only because he didn't know anyone who actually belonged to the Resistance, but also because there were so many different factions, each of which acted on its own.

But that wasn't the real problem for Ali and his family. It was not, as both he and his father realised, a question of talking to people who were actually in the Resistance, but the embarrassment of explaining the reasons for Sameh being detained in the first place. Not many people knew that Sameh was homosexual; and those who knew preferred to ignore it, or at least never to mention it unless they were angry with him. "But what would you expect from a queer?" they would ask themselves, or others, when Sameh did something that upset them. And what could you tell them?

Years later when we met at Heathrow Airport, Ali asked himself the same question: "What can you tell people?"

He was distressed and looked as if he were re-living the events of that evening and the following days after. His father and he, he said, knew that on no account could they go around inquiring whether Sameh had actually been detained. People who knew Sameh would probably have thought it was about time that the queer got straightened out. As for those who didn't know him very well, who didn't know his secret, they were bound to assume that he was being detained because he was a collaborator, or at least suspected of being a collaborator. No smoke without fire, people would say; and of course when everything was made public, after Sameh had been killed, they said that and more.

"We waited, my father and I," said Ali. "We waited that night hoping that Sameh might turn up and then we would realise that we had just been victims of three swindlers. But it was getting very late and there was no sign of Sameh. Of course it was a false hope from the beginning. It wasn't usual for Sameh to stay out late at night, especially when there was a curfew."

"You were the one who used to stay out late," I said, trying both to remind him of those evenings we spent at Hajj Ramadan's café and to divert his mind from painful memories.

But it seemed to me that he very much wanted to recall what had happened before he left Lebanon seventeen years earlier. He had never talked about that before, he said. There was nobody to talk to. Besides, he said, in America he never felt the need to talk about the past. It just seemed to fade away the moment he reached

Michigan, and within a couple of years, it seemed more like an unresolved part of his life. Of course he was worried that the Arab community there would know about his past, he said. He was particularly worried that they would find out that he had been an Israeli collaborator, and he had to deal with this.

"I talked to the imam of the mosque," he said, "and once I talked to him it became like an unsettled account."

It was funny to hear him say that, because that was more or less how I felt about the past a short time after arriving in London. I didn't think of the past as an unresolved, so much as an unreal, episode, a dream that I had been through.

"Probably because our life back in Lebanon felt temporary," I said, reflecting on my own sense of the past, and trying at the same time to urge him to tell me some more about his.

"It was easy to forget it, or to ignore it, because we felt we didn't belong there," he said, "I mean, it was too long to be considered a temporary life."

"It wasn't temporary, but it felt as if it were temporary," I said, "the fact that we didn't feel that we belonged made us feel that we were living there temporarily."

Ali didn't seem convinced, but he didn't say anything in reply. He was eager to get back to what had happened that night when Sameh was arrested. He was in the mood to recollect past events and probably didn't want to analyse his perception of those days for fear of spoiling such a mood. And who could blame him, I thought? He had not had the opportunity to get things off his chest before. He was feeling guilty and he wanted to talk: the memory of his brother must have tormented him all these years.

"Of course I didn't forget Sameh or my family for one second," he said suddenly, "but I forgot the past as one whole chapter, including the events of that night. Up to now I didn't want to remember it."

The hope of Sameh coming home that night turned out to be a false hope, as Ali and his father had thought from the beginning. By two o'clock in the morning Ali and his father had had to resign themselves to the fact that Sameh was actually detained and that the three men who came to them were from the Resistance.

"They were from the Resistance," Abu Ali said as if declaring a formal end to their hope.

To Ali's dismay his father made this declaration with a discernible sense of relief. It didn't feel as if he had painfully resigned himself to the fact that Sameh had actually been detained but rather that he preferred it that way. He must have hoped that Sameh might give up his shameful behaviour, or would at least stay away for a while from the neighbourhood where he was seen and known for what he was.

Ali was extremely angry with his father and nearly had a fight with him for showing so little concern for Sameh's fate. But no sooner had he realised that than deep down he himself felt the same way; that it might have been for the best that Sameh had been compelled to work for the Resistance.

Sameh was an embarrassment to Ali, as much as he was to his parents and the rest of the family. Ali always tried to avoid talking about him. Whenever Maher and I mentioned Sameh's name in our conversation a look of unease appeared on Ali's face, and he would hasten to change the subject. Both Maher and I were aware that Sameh was a homosexual but we pretended that we didn't know. However, we believed that sooner or later something would happen to Sameh. He was often seen with other men going to deserted houses used mainly by drug addicts and homosexuals. We believed that he was going to be targeted by one group or another who claimed to uphold moral standards. When it came to upholding moral standards, we thought, everybody pretended to be their champion, and no one would come out in defence of a homosexual. We nearly warned Ali that he and his parents should do something about it before it was too late.

And when Sameh was killed, and subsequently Ali and his father were arrested, I regretted not talking to Ali about it – even though Ali might not have appreciated it.

And that morning when I went with Maher's brothers to Ali's house and saw how worried he was, I assumed that he already knew that Maher was missing. But when I told him and he responded by saying "Maher as well?" I assumed that something must have happened to Sameh too. Of course I didn't know for sure until weeks later when Sameh was shot dead. Up until that moment I was worried and shocked about Maher's disappearance and brutal murder.

"Maher as well?" I remembered him saying while retreating into the apartment with an unexpected move, as if he had been swept by a sudden gust. We were standing at the doorstep and I felt that at any moment he might fall down.

"Are you all right?" I asked and rushed to hold him, but he quickly moved aside in a gesture of inviting us in. "Yes! I'm all right!" he replied. We went into the sitting room. The apartment was silent and at first I thought Ali was alone. But as soon as he went to the kitchen to make coffee I heard some whispering.

First I heard his father asking: "Do they know anything?" And then I heard Ali replying: "No they don't. It's Maher! He's gone missing!" And Abu Ali said something, which I didn't catch, but to which I heard Ali responding: "No need for these kind of remarks right now!"

I expected Abu Ali to come in and talk to Maher's brothers and me. He often talked to me when I visited, and he quite often warned us, Ali and me, against the risk of Maher's friendship. He didn't like Maher because Maher showed political interests and always pretended to belong to a political party. He also believed that Ali and I were gullible and impulsive young men who would soon fall into trouble under the bad influence of someone like Maher.

But that morning, when I went there with Maher's two brothers, Abu Ali didn't come to talk to me. I thought he probably would have liked to tell me that he had always known that Maher was trouble, and that his sudden disappearance was the result of his reckless talk and behaviour, but because of Maher's brothers he must have preferred to stay away.

Soon Ali came back and we all sat there, sipping our coffee in silence, and from time to time looking at one another helplessly. I thought that Ali was too distracted to be of any help in our search for Maher and I decided that we should leave as soon as we had finished our coffee.

Maher's brothers were eager to hear something comforting about their brother. Once or twice they asked Ali where he would advise them to go next. Ali gave no clear answers and I thought that we must immediately go on our way. The two brothers were extremely nervous and I wanted to reassure them that no effort was being spared.

As we rose to leave, Ali suggested that he accompany us. At least, he said, he could ask those who might know something about their missing brother. Ali knew quite a few people and he certainly could have been very helpful; but in the circumstances I thought at first that his suggestion was due only to a reluctant sense of duty. However, I soon realised that he actually wanted to look for Maher as well, and from then up to the moment when we learned that Maher's body had been found on the eastern route out of the city, he rarely left us. Though he remained distracted, he seemed to be doing his best to be helpful.

It was funny to see Ali being so continuously distracted when normally it was I who had rarely been able to pay enough attention to what was being said and done. Ali himself used to get angry with me. "You are weird, you are!" he used to tell me. "Someone is talking to you and you look as if you're on another planet." Now, I said to myself, it was he who couldn't be focused, he who kept biting his fingernails, and he who in familiar parts of the city suddenly didn't know which direction was the proper one. I knew that, unlike me, Ali's state of distraction was motivated by an actual worry. What I didn't know then for sure was that that distraction would end only when Sameh was killed, and Ali was arrested and consequently compelled to become an Israeli collaborator, all that before he finally managed to leave for America via Ben-Gurion Airport.

Remembering what had happened, I thought that Ali's state of distraction back then was like a sign of the nightmare to follow. For in a matter of a few weeks Ali's life was turned upside down. He changed so much that for me he had become practically unrecognisable. And when I met him years later, at Heathrow Airport, at first it was as if I were meeting someone who had returned from the dead. In spite of all that had happened to him over seventeen years, in spite of the American accent and expressions, that day I met him at Heathrow, I felt that this was the real Ali. He was, I said to myself, the Ali I knew up till that night when the four of us were together for the last time. As for the subsequent events, on that very night after we had left the café, and in the days and weeks that followed, they kept appearing to me as a nightmare in chronological order. First there were George's surprisingly intimate confessions which, in the light of what happened next, could have been seen as a sign of what was to come. Then there was the detention of Sameh, the disappearance of Maher and the death of both of them. All that was followed by the arrest of Ali and his father whose detention didn't end until Ali agreed to become an Israeli collaborator. The nightmare came to its conclusion only when Ali managed to flee.

I saw very little of Ali after Maher's death. On the few occasions when we did meet he looked distant and we hardly said anything to each other. And after he became an Israeli collaborator we stopped seeing one another: Ali made sure that we didn't meet. He felt ashamed of what he had become, yet he also didn't want to involve me in his troubles. He thought that if people saw us together they would believe that I had become a collaborator too. People back then fed on rumours and Ali decided to stop meeting me.

In turn I myself avoided him. It was sad but I had to do it not only because I too was frightened that people might think that I had become a collaborator, but also because everything changed for me after George's confession and the shocking death of Maher. Something had broken, and I felt that it was time to part company.

Besides, Ali was totally engrossed in his worry over his brother. For days after Sameh was held by the Resistance and made to work for them, Ali kept expecting to hear some frightening news. At any moment Sameh might be caught smuggling weapons.

Ali was not only worried for Sameh but for his father and himself too. He knew that if the Israelis caught Sameh smuggling weapons in a van that belonged to the family business they would come to take revenge on the whole family, which was exactly what they did do after Sameh's death.

Sameh was driving the van on the coastal road towards Tyre when he was shot. The van was full of ammunition, and Sameh suddenly found himself approaching an Israeli checkpoint. It was not, as he soon realised, one of those checkpoints where cars were routinely waved on, but one through which no car was allowed to pass until it had been thoroughly searched. It could be a random car search, Sameh thought, or possibly the Israelis had been informed of his mission. But whatever it was, the Israelis were bound to search the van and find the ammunition. He didn't know what to do. He couldn't just keep driving right up to the checkpoint, but neither could he turn back without arousing the soldiers' suspicions. He panicked and without knowing exactly what he was doing, he stopped, switched off the engine, got out and rushed towards a nearby orchard. But before he managed to disappear into the orchard he was seen and pursued by soldiers. It was the driver of the car behind him who saw him first. He shouted at Sameh not to leave his van in the middle of the road, and then the Israeli soldiers noticed what was happening and ran after him.

Days, or perhaps weeks later, that driver was arrested and questioned by the Resistance. He swore that he did not know that Sameh was working for the Resistance. He burst into tears, saying that he regretted the fact that he had shouted at him. He wished, he said, that he had lost his tongue at that very moment. He had thought that Sameh had stopped the car in order to relieve himself, not to run away from the Israelis. And had he known that the man belonged to the Resistance he would have waited until Sameh had managed to get as far away as possible before alerting the Israelis to the van which was parked in the middle of the road without a driver.

He was clearly frightened that his interrogators, all armed men from the Resistance, would accuse him of working for the Israelis. He didn't stop crying and apologising, and swore that had he known, he would have gone out of his way to point the Israelis in the opposite direction in order to give Sameh a greater chance of getting away.

But whether the driver was telling the truth or lying, the fact of the matter was that Sameh had been pursued into the orchard and shot at. Two bullets hit him while he was running and he fell dead – instantly.

Later that day, when the Israelis discovered the identity of both Sameh and the owner of the van, two military vehicles and one civilian car pulled up in front of Ali's building. Soldiers and officers of the Israeli intelligence services jumped out and surrounded it. One intelligence officer backed by three soldiers knocked at the front door, and when it was opened they rushed in shouting, ordering everybody to stand with their face to the wall. Ali, his parents, his two young sisters and youngest brother stood in the sitting room with their face to the wall while soldiers and intelligence officers searched every corner of the house. Eventually they turned to Ali and his father. The pair were blindfolded, dragged into the back seat of the waiting car and driven off.

"I was so frightened, I thought they were going to kill us," Ali said to me when we met at Heathrow Airport.

"Israelis didn't shoot people like that!" I said.

"Didn't they?"

"Well, they weren't like other groups who kidnapped people and shot them!" I said. "Look at what happened to Maher!"

Ali looked at me quizzically, trying to work out exactly what I was trying to say. He knew that Israelis didn't kidnap people and shoot them, but that didn't mean that it was totally unreasonable of him to worry that the Israelis might have shot him and his father, especially when they were blindfolded and taken away. He must have suspected that I was trying to say something else, and actually I was.

From the moment we met I felt that, after all those years, I ought to spare him any sense of shame for his past as an Israeli collaborator. I wanted to assure him that I had grown indifferent enough to see past events from a totally objective point of view, that now it meant very little what people had or hadn't done back then. But it seemed that Ali himself no longer felt a sense of shame. He had grown to look at what had happened with some detachment.

"It was a mess!" he said.

"It still is!" I agreed.

He nodded and told me that throughout all those years in Michigan, there was something that he kept remembering every time he heard anything about the situation in the Middle East. It was the last interesting thing that he had heard before he left the region.

He was on his way from Lebanon to Israel where he was supposed to fly on to America. It was the only way for him to get out of Lebanon before the Israelis withdrew from our area. He was driven by an Israeli soldier assigned to help him get as far as Tel Aviv. They were silent most of the way. Ali was sad to go, especially as he had assumed that he might never come back again, while the soldier didn't seem to have anything to say to him. But as soon as they got close to the airport, the soldier looked at him and told him that he was lucky to be leaving. Ali nodded with approval, and thought of saying that anybody who managed to leave Lebanon then, must consider himself lucky.

"I wish I could leave too!" the soldier said.

"Why?" Ali asked, "Wouldn't it be enough for you to return home?"

"The whole region is a mess," he replied, "Lebanon, Israel, everywhere around here is in a mess!"

Ali didn't know whether to agree with the soldier or not. Deep down he believed that the soldier was right, yet he suspected that he was being quizzed and decided to remain silent.

"It's a mess," the Israeli soldier went on, this time in a low voice as if he were talking to himself, "and it will never be right until everybody gives up!"

"Everybody gives up!" Ali repeated the words of the soldier as if to encourage him to explain what he meant.

"If everybody stops giving a damn," he said, "you know, when every side stops being concerned about what the other side is up to."

Ali nodded. If only everybody would give up! He thought he had given up, but others didn't and wouldn't, and that's why he had to end up going to America via Israel.

"It was a mess!" said Ali when we met at Heathrow Airport. "A total mess and Sameh and Maher were two of its victims," he added, trying to explain to me why he no longer felt ashamed for having become an Israeli collaborator.

It's true, I said to myself. It was a mess, and Sameh and Maher were its victims. They were victims, I said to myself, but what about Amina? I knew that I must tell Ali about Amina. I must tell him what he didn't know, I said to myself – what nobody knew apart from us, my parents, my brother, and me.

Now was the right time to tell Ali about Amina, I said to myself, and so I began.

5

It was the last night when the four of us were together.

That night I thought of my sister Amina, and in the morning, just before Maher's brothers came to tell me that Maher had not come home the night before, I told my mother that I had been thinking of Amina. This was the first time that I told anybody that I had been thinking about Amina. For quite a long time I had wished to mention Amina's name to my mother – not only to mention her name but also to talk at length about her. But I never dared till that morning. And it must have been the result of what had happened the day before: first it was something that mother said when she casually mentioned Amina. She was talking about the year when it snowed. "I think it was the year when I was pregnant with Amina," she said and fell into a sudden, deep silence. At once I understood the cause of that silence. It was a long time since I had heard mother talking about Amina. She rarely mentioned her name, and certainly never in front of either father or brother Kamal. They had forbidden her from talking about her deceased daughter.

And later that night, after Maher left the café, George and I took a stroll. He told me about his family. George's revelations urged me to make my own, and the only revelation I had to divulge was what had happened to Amina. At the beginning I thought that I owed it to George, as a friend who was entrusting me with the secrets of his private life, to tell him some secrets of my own. When it turned out that George didn't tell me what he did in order to strengthen the bond of friendship between us, I nevertheless still wanted to talk about Amina. I realised that I only wanted to talk about Amina.

I had been waiting to find someone to whom I could tell what had happened, and that night George seemed the perfect listener. But George was more eager to talk than to listen. He certainly didn't want to divert attention from his story to mine. He probably wanted his story to be the only one to be told at that moment, he wanted it to be the story that would bring our friendship to an end.

Nevertheless I felt I had to talk about Amina, and the next morning I told mother that I had thought of Amina. Mother looked at me first with surprise, but soon she turned her face aside, and burst into tears. It was not the first time that I had seen mother cry when Amina was mentioned. Since Kamal had left for Saudi Arabia and I had started to spend most of my time outside the house, mother had got into the habit of weeping every time something was said that reminded her of Amina. And to be honest, I could not help feeling a sense of satisfaction whenever that happened.

It seemed that mother had conceded the truth of what had happened to her only daughter, that after ten years she realised that the death of Amina was a greater loss than she had ever feared. Now, I thought, she must have realised that a whole world was stolen from her, a daughter who could have helped her and with whom she could have shared a lot of things – a daughter who would have been by now a married woman whom she could proudly visit and talk about to her neighbours and friends.

Ten years ago Amina was only seventeen, merely a girl playing a part in a play that involved my parents and our world. Amina was groomed to be the epitome of the new Palestinian woman, not the wife or the mother who minded the house and children, but the comrade and partner of the Palestinian man in the so-called "national struggle". Amina, my fair-haired sister, was groomed to be "Comrade Amina", an icon Palestinian women would look up to and in whose footsteps they would follow.

And she went along with this big lie with great enthusiasm. She was not the only one; other girls of the same age and neighbourhood believed that they represented the new Palestinian woman who was fighting the political battle side by side with Palestinian men. Like her, they were deceived, yet they were not as unfortunate as she was.

Years later when I met Ali at Heathrow Airport and told him how Amina had died, I couldn't help remembering what had happened during the funeral. "On the day of Amina's funeral," I said to Ali, "her female comrades looked as if her death had forced them to see the shocking reality of their society."

That afternoon when I met Ali at Heathrow and listened to him recalling how his brother Sameh was killed, I realised that this was the time to tell somebody about my sister Amina. Ali knew about Amina from before, but he didn't know that she had actually killed herself. He believed that it was an accident, or, as many suspected, that she was killed. Now, I thought, after so many years and after we had talked openly about his brother Sameh, I must tell him about Amina. He was stunned.

"Amina's friends, or comrades, as they were called, were shocked," I said, "and they realised that they were no better than the old Palestinian women, if not worse. There was no new Palestinian woman after all."

Yes, I said, some of them managed to go along with the explanation which was given for Amina's death, they willingly accepted the lie and the deception. Most, however, were too bewildered to retreat into self-deception. And when the leader of the Women's Organisation to which they belonged stood up at Amina's funeral and made a speech in which she praised Amina for dying whilst performing her duty, they let out the most horrific screams and wails that were ever heard in our neighbourhood. It was so shocking that the leader of the Women's Organisation could not help blushing in shame.

At the time I didn't realise exactly what had happened to make them interrupt their own leader in that way. At first I thought that they loved Amina so much that they couldn't prevent themselves from expressing their painful grief in such an appalling manner, making their leader stop and look ashamed. But later I realised that they were expressing both grief and a sense of protest against the lie in which the death of Amina, and their own lives, had been shrouded. They had believed that Amina had been killed. And when the leader, in her speech, praised Amina for her courage in falling as "a martyr while she was performing her revolutionary duty," they knew that that was a blatant lie, and so they could not help screaming and wailing in protest. But they could not put an end to the lie. Their embarrassing screaming and wailing came to nothing. The leader went on with her speech, and within a week huge colourful posters appeared on the walls of the Camp heralding Amina as the "heroine martyr who died while fighting the Zionist enemy".

"You remember those posters?" I asked Ali. "Every time someone who belonged to a faction died, a photo would appear on posters glued to the walls of the Camp heralding him as a hero martyr."

"Yes! I remember," said Ali, and then added sarcastically, "even if he had died in a car accident!"

"Or as in Amina's case," I said. But just before I completed the sentence I stopped. I didn't want to say, "took her own life", not just yet. It was too early to make such a revelation, I thought to myself.

"Or like Amina," I hastened to modify my statement. "She wasn't a martyr!"

Everybody knew what the poster claimed was a lie. But we were living many lies, then. And when I thought about it, years later, I felt disappointed that Amina had been deceived so easily by such lies. How could she have been so stupid as to believe what she was told, to take it so seriously? But then I realised that it was not the politics that had drawn Amina into joining the Women's Organisation, nor was it the rhetoric about the so-called new Palestinian woman – which was what in reality the politics amounted to anyway. Rather it was the work itself.

Joining the Women's Organisation was a way for her to

be able to go out and do something, and certainly not to end up the way so many other Palestinian women did. She had actually believed, I said to myself, that she could use the Organisation, or to be precise the lie that the Organisation represented, in order to get her own way.

"She took a huge risk," I told Ali, "she thought that she could do anything if she pretended that she believed the rhetoric. What she didn't realise was that they, I mean my parents, my brother Kamal and her leader in the Women's Organisation, didn't believe it any more than she did."

Ali nodded. He looked a bit embarrassed and I assumed that he must have been feeling the same way I had when he had spoken about his brother.

"I thought Americans were quite keen on revelations and confessions," I said sarcastically. "Perhaps you haven't become American enough."

"No, not American enough!" he said, "Mind you, a lot of Americans are quite reticent. Nor do they like to know about other people's problems."

I knew what he meant but I was not going to be diverted from talking about Amina now that I had started. I hastened to make it clear to him that we were not going to get off this subject before I had finished everything I wanted to say.

"You see, mother didn't always show grief over Amina," I said to Ali, "but that morning, when I told her that I had been thinking of Amina, she was genuinely sad and wept silently."

Ten years earlier, when Amina killed herself, mother

was more ashamed than sad. "How could she do such a thing?" I remember her asking herself just after we had come out of the room in which Amina had taken her own life. The devastating sight of Amina, lying on the floor with eyes wide open, blood splattered all over the floor and furniture, horrified mother, but it did not seem to be horrific enough for her not to think of the shame that this incident would bring upon us. She knew that nobody would believe that Amina had killed herself because her eldest brother bullied and humiliated her: no young woman reacted in such a way. Older family members didn't bully or humiliate their youngest – they merely did what they were entitled to do for the benefit of the young.

Whenever Amina complained that Kamal was bullying her, my parents dismissed what they perceived as sheer girls' indulgence. "There's nothing wrong with your brother keeping an eye on you, or telling you what to do!" "Nothing wrong with him hitting you if you've done something wrong! It's for your own good!" "Good thing that you have an older brother who cares! You should be grateful, even if he hits you!" my parents would tell Amina and me every time we complained about Kamal. And on more than one occasion my father related how his own eldest brother hit him with a shoe. "I was already a married man, and yet I didn't dare say a word of protest out of pure respect. Respect for my brother, the eldest!" my father said. "That was the kind of education we received in those days!"

He was proud of that kind of education, and expected

us to be proud too. When Amina took her own life he was totally baffled. He never did understand why, I told Ali. Mother, on the other hand, did seem to understand but was more worried about what the neighbours might say.

"In our neighbourhood, in our society in general, as you well know, a woman did not kill herself unless she had done something gravely shameful," I said to Ali in a tone of voice in which I tried to sound as sarcastic as possible. "Namely, if she got pregnant or lost her virginity before marriage."

Mother was unable to ignore what people would think and say. She cried for her daughter, she cried for weeks, yet at the same time she could not help being over-whelmed by that profound sense of shame. "How could she do this to us?" she wondered, and when father and my brother Kamal suggested claiming that it was an accident, mother looked relieved. It was only then that she was able to cry and wail freely over her seventeen-year-old daughter. She was devastated, I said to Ali, there had been no doubt about it; she mourned her Amina, and wore black for months. Nevertheless on the day Kamal and father suggested that the best thing for us was to claim that Amina died while she was cleaning her pistol, mother was sober enough to appreciate such a convenient explanation for her daughter's death. And when the leader of the Women's Organisation attended the funeral and made that speech in which she described Amina as an example of the "New Palestinian Woman", and that her death was a high form of self-sacrifice, I felt that mother could not help being proud. She cried, but in a way restrained enough to show that she believed that her daughter had not died in vain.

Yes, at that moment she was willing to deceive herself and believe that her daughter was truly a martyr. We were still living in the Camp and we were used to hearing of people dying as martyrs. Nearly every morning we saw a new, huge and cheaply produced colourful poster glued to the walls of houses in the Camp heralding some new martyr or other. We knew that many of those so-called martyrs had very little to do with martyrdom or dying in the battlefield. Most people said nothing about it, but some who tended to be shockingly direct and vulgar did not hesitate to make fun of them. And when Amina was declared a martyr they made fun of her too.

A week after Amina's death the Women's Organisation produced one of those colourful posters using a passport photo of Amina. She was described, in that familiar rhetoric of such publications, as a martyr who was killed while fighting the Zionist enemy.

"Hero martyr!" some people said mockingly. "Martyred while fighting the enemy!" they said and laughed. We had told them that Amina died accidentally, not that they believed us; but it was adequate proof that she was not killed "fighting the enemy" as the poster claimed.

"She was killed all right," some said, "but not by the 'Zionist enemy'!"

"The 'Zionist enemy' is innocent of her blood!" they said sarcastically. "It was her own brother!"

It was rumoured that she was pregnant and that Kamal

had to kill her. "And a good thing too," they said, "she had abused the freedom she was given!"

My parents and Kamal were so angry when they heard this. Mother cried, and Kamal swore that if he knew who was behind such a lie he would cut his tongue out. The whole family was enraged. Aunts, uncles and cousins heard the rumour, and came to see whether there was any truth in it. If this was true, one of my aunts warned, it would be harmful to the whole family. She had a marriageable daughter and such talk would cast doubt on her chastity and the chastity of all the daughters of the family. She said that we should all work to repudiate it, but it seemed that some family members were not in too much of a hurry to do so, at least not before making the point that their earlier concerns had been right.

They had objected to Amina being allowed to join the Women's Organisation, and on one occasion they were extremely angry because some friends or neighbours of theirs had seen Amina dressed in a military outfit, carrying a pistol and smoking out in the street. They complained, saying that if my parents were not worried enough about the reputation of Amina, they were worried about their own daughters'. Not only that Amina's behaviour could damage the reputation of her unmarried female cousins but it was also setting a bad example to them. "The other day," one aunt said, "I caught my daughter Aida smoking and when I told her off she protested that her cousin Amina smoked in the street and nobody had said anything." Other aunts and uncles nodded, implying that each one of them had a similar story to tell.

My parents rarely took their criticisms seriously. They looked down on the rest of the family, considering them unnecessarily strict and backward. My parents actually felt flattered: for them such complaints were proof of their own progressive mentality and attitude. They no longer lived by the conventions and customs of their family. They had become educated and enlightened, and had moved on. But in truth my parents, and my brother Kamal (especially my brother Kamal, who a few years later went to Saudi Arabia and became religious), were no more enlightened than the rest of the family; they only wished to appear so. It was their way of giving the impression that they had moved on to a higher class; an impression they not only felt themselves, but also wanted others to notice. It was their unconcealed aim.

The frequent visits of Kamal's comrades to our house gave my parents the chance to feel and behave differently. Kamal was a member of the Democratic Front for the Liberation of Palestine, and most of his comrades were young educated men who treated my parents with great respect. They sat with them and talked to them about politics and revolutions all over the world. In those days people still believed in revolutions and liberation, and Kamal's comrades were very enthusiastic and often talked with great passion about the "progressive societies" – as they put it – in China and Vietnam. They spared no opportunity to criticise our society for being backward and hypocritical, particularly with regard to women. "It's not enough to have a political revolution," they often complained, "we must also have a social revolution!"

"Look at the Chinese women, at the Vietnamese women!" they would declare with great enthusiasm. "What do you see? Liberated women in a liberated society!"

My parents used to listen to all that and feel that they were important, that they had been chosen from among the whole neighbourhood to be told such important things. And it was precisely because of that feeling that they finally permitted Amina to join the Women's Organisation.

My brother Kamal wanted to object, but he could not. After all he had agreed, or at least pretended to agree completely with his comrades that our society could not be liberated before the liberation of women. Besides, the Women's Organisation was part of the DFLP to which he belonged, and he must have felt too embarrassed to forbid his own sister to join his party. At one stage he objected, claiming that she should not be distracted from her studies; it was important for her to pass her exams, he argued, so that she would be ready to go to university. "Education," he claimed in an authoritative tone of voice, "is an important means of liberation for women and society in general!"

He was told that her participation in the Women's Organisation's activities would not clash with her studies; in fact, the Organisation's activities would actually enhance her study and knowledge. So he reluctantly gave in.

"Of course he didn't give a damn about her education," I said to Ali, when I met him at Heathrow Airport and told him the story, "he just wanted to keep bullying her. The 'good Marxist' was worried that if she got into the Women's Organisation she might start standing up to him!"

"Was he a Marxist?" Ali interrupted.

"Well, that's what he called himself," I said, "didn't I tell you before?"

"Maybe, but I must have forgotten! It was such a long time ago. To be honest I don't remember what he looks like."

"Well, he went to Saudi Arabia a long time ago, right at the beginning of the war," I said hesitantly. I wasn't quite sure.

"The beginning of the war? You mean the war of 1975?"

"Yes, but he actually left in 1976, don't you remember?" I said, but I myself was still not certain of the date, "I haven't seen him for twenty-four years now!"

"I know that he left Lebanon a long time ago," Ali said, "I didn't realise it's been twenty-four years."

"Yes!"

"Did he ever return to Lebanon?" Ali asked.

"I don't know," I said, "perhaps after I left. I don't keep in touch with him."

"So, in Lebanon he was a Marxist, but in Saudi Arabia he became an Islamist?" Ali asked sarcastically.

"Not an Islamist, but religious. He went on Hajj and all that!" I said. "He actually invited me to visit him once during the Hajj season, so that I could see him and perform the pilgrimage at the same time."

"Why didn't you?" Ali asked mockingly. "You'd have become a Hajji."

"You are the one who should have been a Hajji!" I said referring to what he had told me about his life in Michigan, "you could do well as a Hajji in America."

"That's all fun, man!" he said switching to English.

"Fun?" I repeated his word in English, and then continued in Arabic: "Be careful that you don't say such a thing in front of the sheikhs in Lebanon!" I said sarcastically. "Our religion is no fun, as you well know!"

"Is he married?" Ali asked in what seemed to me an attempt to change the subject. He was a bit worried about what could happen to him when he got to Lebanon, and he obviously didn't want to be reminded of it.

"He must be married!" Ali went on.

"Yes! He is married and has children, Comrade Kamal!"

"You mean Hajji Kamal?"

"Yes, Hajji Kamal!" I said. "I wonder what his old comrades would think of him now?"

"Whatever happened to them?"

"I don't really know, but I expect some of them went his way, and discovered their 'great religion', as he calls it!"

We were silent for a while. But I still wanted to talk about Amina. There was more to tell, I thought, and without telling it, Amina's story as it stood so far did not sound of any importance. For example, I particularly wanted Ali to know that regardless of my parents' and Kamal's attitude, it was Amina herself who made joining the Women's Organisation a fact.

Weeks before they relented, Amina started going to the Organisation's centre. She introduced herself to the leader of the centre, and talked to other members. She even participated in some of their preliminary activities. By the time my parents and Kamal allowed her to join the organisation, she had practically become a member. They did not know that, and went on instructing her on what she could and couldn't do. They said that she should never stay out later than eight o'clock in the evening, and under no circumstances was she to be alone with her male comrades. Nor should she smoke, laugh loudly or wear anything that drew attention to herself. Their instructions fell on deaf ears, and before long Amina developed the appearance of someone totally different from the person we knew. She started dressing in a guerilla fighter's outfit, carrying a pistol or slinging a kalashnikov over her shoulder, smoking in public, selling the Organisation's weekly paper on the street, and she was rarely seen without the company of one or two of her male comrades. I remembered her image quite clearly. She really looked different – but it didn't take her long to appear so different. It was as if there had always been a different person in her who had been striving to become visible.

My parents felt uneasy but Amina was clever enough to gain their approval, or at least silence. She often brought her comrades round and introduced them to my family in an attempt to make them accepted as friends of my parents and Kamal. Nevertheless she couldn't appease the whole family.

Uncles, aunts and cousins were often outraged by Amina's appearance and behaviour, and some of them kept visiting us, protesting and demanding that she must be stopped. On one occasion they all appeared together and there was a huge row. The previous day they had seen Amina with two of her male comrades going from one shelter to another checking on civilians who were shelter-ing from an Israeli air raid. It was not unusual for members of the Women's Organisation to go around checking on people during such air raids to see if anybody needed help, but it was embarrassing and somehow unfamiliar for some of our aunts and uncles to see their own niece doing such a thing. And what made it even more embarrassing was that their neighbours had recognised Amina too.

Two of my uncles who had actually seen her swore that they would never set foot in our house again unless Amina was prevented from carrying on with all that nonsense and shaming the whole family.

My parents were taken aback by such a threat; they were actually taken aback by the whole meeting. Although they were used to visits from no more than two or three uncles and aunts, never before had they actually been threatened with being cut off.

Nevertheless they were just as eager to use the meeting as an opportunity to display how far they had moved on and how different they had become from the rest of the family. When the aunts and uncles had calmed down, after an outburst of protest, my parents hastened to explain, in an undeniably patronising tone of voice, that times had changed, that civilised people no longer kept their daughters, and women in general, under lock and key.

Of course my parents didn't really mean it, but they looked very happy to have an opportunity to say it. At one point they sounded as if they were trying to outdo one another as to who would make the more pretentious statement. If my father said that civilised people did or didn't behave in this or that manner, my mother hastened to add, "Look at them in France and Italy and Germany!" Once she even mentioned Israel. "How do you think that old bag Golda Meir became prime minister?" she asked. "Do you think that her parents locked her up, and prevented her from joining political organisations?"

"My parents," I told Ali when we were in the airport, "were proud of making such statements, even though in reality the words meant nothing to them. They never mentioned China and Vietnam, which were supposed to be the model for liberating Palestinian women."

"They didn't care much for revolutionary models, I suppose!" Ali said sarcastically.

"That's true," I said, "but also because our relatives would've laughed at them! 'China and Vietnam?' they would've said, 'what do we have to imitate those starving people for?'"

As it happened our relatives never calmed down no matter what country was mentioned. They certainly did not like it when my mother mentioned Israel. "What! You are hoping now that your daughter will become a Golda Meir?" one uncle asked sarcastically, and then they all started talking at the same time again.

Some of them turned to Kamal. Up to that moment Kamal had been silent, and they assumed, rightly so, that his silence was a sign of endorsing their complaints. Kamal had never sincerely approved of Amina joining the Women's Organisation, and he certainly didn't appreciate the way she dressed and behaved since she had become a member. Fearing that his comrades would accuse him of being backward, or a hypocrite, which he was, he could not prevent her from joining up. Still he was always waiting for an opportunity to make her life hard. And the day when the whole family came to protest Amina's behaviour, Kamal realised that here was another chance for him to bully her. Promising to put an end to her reckless behaviour, he told our angry visitors that there was nothing wrong about Amina working with the Women's Organisation. "It is her national duty," he said. And after a pause he added, "However, doing her national duty is no excuse for her to forget her duty to protect her reputation and the reputation of the women in our family."

"That's exactly what we are talking about," said one of the uncles with a great sense of relief. They were all pleased, and went on nodding in approval.

"She must learn that she has a family to reckon with!" Kamal went on, probably encouraged by their approval.

"Well said!" they nodded again. Of course they would have felt even more relieved had Kamal promised to make her quit the Women's Organisation altogether, but they knew that it would have been too embarrassing for him to do so. What Kamal said was satisfactory enough for them.

At least they could leave less angry than when they had come. At last they had found an ally who could put their worries to rest. Kamal was their man, and he certainly was more than happy to keep an eye on Amina in the name of protecting the family's reputation, to tell her off whenever she seemed to have crossed the line of acceptable behaviour. And according to his concept of "acceptable behaviour", nothing that Amina did could be tolerated. Smoking in public, staying out late, arguing with her comrades in a loud voice, accompanying her male comrades, practically everything that Amina did, everything warranted his intervention and him telling her off. He didn't only tell her off; on more than one occasion he thumped her, and prevented her from going out. My parents did intervene when they thought that he was being too harsh. They were mostly on his side though. They believed profoundly that men had authority over women, and the old over the young. Yet they were also anxious to maintain their pretence at being progressive parents.

When Kamal was not able to do exactly what he wished, he grew ever more frustrated, but given that he was keeping a close eye on Amina, waiting for her to take a wrong step, his frustration didn't last long. Every day he followed her to the centre in the hope of catching her in a compromising position – and eventually he did just that.

Inside the centre, he caught her kissing a male comrade. He was happy and shocked, happy because at last he had obtained the excuse that he wanted in order to make her quit the Organisation, and shocked to see his own sister kissing a strange man. He often thought that she was capable of doing only what uncles and aunts believed to be shameful, but he did not really think she would actually do anything. Yet there she was, kissing someone. He stood there looking at her, unable to believe what he was seeing. "Amina!" he cried out, and had Amina not moved away from the young man she was kissing, Kamal would have remained standing there looking at her as if he were looking at a perfect stranger. As soon as he noticed that she had moved away, he quickly rushed towards her, blocking her escape as if he wanted to keep all the evidence at the scene of the crime.

She tried to force her way past him, but he pushed her back and started hitting and kicking her. "Bitch! Bitch!" he snarled while grabbing her by the hair. He seemed to want to drag her by the hair out on to the street and all the way home. It seemed that he wanted people to see him dragging her so that everybody would believe that she had done something wrong. Mercifully her young friend moved in to stop Kamal. He had no chance, but his attempt was enough to compel Kamal to let go of Amina. She took the opportunity to break free and run out of the centre and back home.

Kamal followed her immediately. He was anxious to arrive home before she had the chance to tell my parents her side of the story and deny the fact that she had kissed a man. He did not realise that Amina was feeling too humiliated to deny anything or even to talk. She was humiliated in front of the man she obviously loved and didn't much care about denying anything. Crying out of shame, she rushed into her room and locked the door from the inside.

My mother and I were sitting on the terrace, which spread out in front of the house. We were both surprised to see her appearing in that state and at once mother thought some relative of ours must have died. Mother often thought that some friend or relative had died in circumstances such as these. As we rushed to Amina's room Kamal appeared, breathless and angry, swearing that he would kill her before she brought shame on the family.

"The bitch! I'll kill her!" he shouted again and again.

Mother was terrified to hear him calling Amina a bitch. It was quite unusual for Kamal or any member of the family to call his sister or any woman in the family a bitch. Mother must have thought that something really shameful had happened. But she could not believe that her daughter was capable of doing something that would shame the family. She tried to calm Kamal down, begging him to stop saying such things, at least not at the top of his voice. She was worried that the neigbhours would hear him, and then Amina's reputation would be ruined forever. Kamal did not calm down and had no intention of doing so. He wanted to remain angry in order to assert forcefully that he had been right all along, and that from then on she should do whatever he thought was right for her and the family. He went on and on, ranting about our shit family until we heard a shot coming from Amina's room.

"Oh, my God!" my mother screamed. Kamal and I forced the door open while mother screamed again. And there was Amina, lying on the floor covered with blood. She had killed herself – with one bullet to the head.

"And do you know what were the first words that came to my mind?" I said to Ali, when I told him the story, "she's pulled the trigger. Amina could pull the trigger!"

It was an answer to Kamal's earlier question: "Can you pull the trigger Amina? Can you pull it?" I remembered Kamal asking her, teasing her the day she came back carrying a pistol. "Can you pull the trigger Comrade Amina? Can you?" he asked teasingly. "Do you have the courage to do it?"

"She did," I said to Ali, and fell silent. We both fell silent.

III Epilogue from the Present

Since the start of this month I have been waiting for the day of the 27th. The closer it gets, the more I have become aware of the fact that it will soon be exactly fifteen years since I left Lebanon. I have been here for fifteen years, that's fifteen years without ever going back, nor seeing any of the people that I used to know then, I kept telling myself with an unmistakable sense of achievement.

But today is Tuesday the 24th, and things have changed. This morning I got up at nine o'clock, which was a bit early for me, and got ready to go to Heathrow Airport. Ali was coming today and I had promised to meet him. The thought of seeing him after all these years felt exciting but also uncomfortable, so much so that it made me unable to decide how I should greet him. Should I behave as if nothing had changed, I asked myself? Should I pretend that I am still the same person he knew seventeen years ago, or should I make sure he realises at once that I am now a totally different person?

I asked myself these questions, and all the way to the airport I tried to settle on an answer. Actually I had tormented myself with such questions ever since the moment I received his phone call ten days ago. It was the first time Ali had got in touch with me. He had contacted me now, I said to myself, only because he was going back to Lebanon. He could have phoned me any time in the last fifteen years but no, he only wanted to get in touch on his return to Lebanon. It seemed to me that I was one of the people whom he intended to see on his visit back to the world of the past. And though I was excited about meeting him after all these years, I certainly didn't want him to consider me as just one of the people from that world. The past had become more like an unreal episode in my mind, I said to myself with a slight tinge of bitterness, and my life over the last fifteen years had been real – real, as I had never experienced reality before.

Ali, I determined, on my way to Heathrow Airport, must understand that I was not George or any of the others who were stuck back there, one who had remained there doing nothing but waiting for those who had left to come back and tell them exciting things. He must understand, I said to myself, and I could not help feeling angry, he must understand that he was not the only one who had left. I too had left. I am one of those who were lucky enough to have left.

It was important to me to be seen as someone who had managed to leave. The thought of people back there talking about me with admiration that I had left was no small consolation especially at times when I was totally alone and without money. Besides, I had often thought that people were of two kinds, those who left and those who stayed. And I, as I often reflected with unusual self-admiration, belonged to the first kind.

It was an idea which I had learned from my sister Amina. It was she who told me that it was natural for people to leave. "People who have any sense, who care about themselves and the world, do not stay," she told me, "they leave!" And naturally she herself belonged to those who left. Her early death was a form of leaving, of getting out as early as possible. And it was precisely her early death that confirmed my most profound fears, of being left behind after everybody had gone away. The thought of people moving away, leaving behind them nothing but a sudden and frightful emptiness, made me panic-stricken and compelled me to think of leaving at the earliest opportunity.

Ali must understand, I thought while travelling on my way to meet him, that I wasn't one of those sad people who stayed behind. I must prove to him that I was not one of those who were eagerly going to receive him and listen to him telling them what he had seen and done in America. I have moved on, I said to myself, just like he has.

I knew, however, that asserting such a fact was not my only concern. I was also worried that Ali might ask me about my present life, namely what I had done and had been doing since I came to London. And what have I achieved? I asked myself with a profound sense of embarrassment. It was the first time that I had felt so embarrassed, which made me suddenly feel awkward about meeting Ali. Ali was sure to discover that most of what I have done was at best a half achievement, I said to myself. And that was enough for him to see it as no more than a sign of total failure. What upset me most was the certain fact that Ali was bound to make my failure publicly known back in Lebanon. I could just imagine the bastard shaking his head, and telling those who asked about me: "He's a loser, man!"

It's not that people back there were under the impression that I have had a successful life, apart from being successful in leaving, but neither did they know that it was a failure. I had managed to keep far enough away from them that either my success or failure had become of little interest to anybody. But now, I thought, Ali goes back and tells them that he has met me, and they are bound to get inquisitive about my life. And of course, he will shake his head and say: "He's a loser, man!"

And I am sure quite a few of them will be happy to agree with him. "We always thought he was a useless sod!" they will say, gloating.

I wish I hadn't come, I thought as I arrived at Heathrow. Why on earth did I have to come? I felt totally oblivious to the hustle and bustle of Heathrow. What did I have to do with someone with whom I no longer had anything in common, apart from a fading past?

These questions grated on me, so much so I nearly turned back. Nevertheless I didn't. I was curious, and I also wished to see if I had actually managed to become as disinterested towards anything from the past as I had been telling myself I was. In other words, it was supposed to be a real test for me. There was also the expectation, perhaps even the hope, of meeting someone slightly shy and hesitant, someone who for the last seventeen years had suffered from a state of withdrawal and loneliness and for whom the sight of an old friend would come as a sign of redemption. Of course I knew that I was projecting my own self-image on him, and so I was not totally surprised when Ali appeared contrary to my expectations. He looked lively, forthcoming and seemingly had very few worries about anything.

"There you are!" he exclaimed the moment he caught a glimpse of me, and rushed to hug me.

I tried to look as reserved as possible, but that didn't hold him back, and he showered me with all sorts of questions in an unmistakably American accent.

"You've become old!" I said, in a dry tone of voice, looking at the bald patch on the top of his head.

"So have you, man!" he said pointing at my grey hair.

"So have I!" I said, hoping that he would realise that I was trying to draw his attention to the fact that we were no longer the same two friends we had been a long time ago. By acknowledging our considerable physical changes, I thought, I could make him aware of the total change in our lives, thus making it clear from the beginning that our meeting was going to be strictly about the past.

"I suppose we've had different ways of life!" I said, making a further remark, and led the way to a café in the arrival area.

"God! We have!" he said mirthfully.

"It's a little bit different from Ramadan Café!" I said in an attempt to start talking about the past right away. And for the next few minutes I kept making hints of this sort in the hope that there would be no room left for mentioning the present. But it seemed that he couldn't help but talk about the present, though to my relief, he didn't seem to be too curious or interested in my life in London. It seemed that he himself had not done too well in America. He must have refrained from inquiring about my life, I thought, in order to avoid talking about his. The only question he asked about my personal life was whether I was married. I told him that I wasn't, and he looked pleased.

"Best thing, man!" he said, and went on to tell me about his ten years of marriage, which had ended in a sad way.

"Different cultures," he said in English, "it's difficult!"

Not you as well! I thought to myself. I have heard this excuse so often that it was the last thing I wanted to hear again, and especially not from Ali. Everyone who fails to keep up a marriage tells me that it's all down to "different cultures". Noticing how unsympathetic I looked, Ali went on saying that it was really difficult for two people from different backgrounds to get on together. He started telling me all about his troubles with his ex-wife, how they picked on one another due to their different cultures. He went on and on about this until I nearly became dizzy. In fact, it seemed that I could hear him saying nothing but those words: "Different cultures! Different cultures!"

Different cultures, I wanted to protest, was balls! I wanted to tell him that people start picking on one another because they stop loving each other, that if the so-called "different cultures" was the determining factor for relationships, how come that he managed to live with his ex-wife for ten years? Where were the different cultures then? I thought of asking him, and before allowing him to answer I wanted to say that that meaningless concept "different cultures" is just an excuse for people to avoid facing themselves and their shortcomings. I wanted to say that there was nothing harder for people than to keep up lasting relationships, and nothing easier than to disagree, regardless of their culture. I thought of reminding him of how profoundly we had disagreed with our

138

own families. I thought of saying this while remembering my brother Kamal, the sight of whom I could never stand. And not only Kamal, come to think of it: there were so many people whom I remembered going to great lengths to avoid talking to, people I didn't even want to see. I wanted to tell Ali all that, but I didn't. I didn't want to argue with him. I thought that if I argued, it would sound as if I cared, and I certainly wanted to preserve an attitude of disinterest. His talk about his failed marriage and his mention of some intimate details had made me feel embarrassed and nervous. Come to think of it now, I believe it was his revealing such intimate details about his marriage that made me more upset than the fact that he had used the term, "different cultures". I assumed that Ali had acquired that peculiar American habit of revealing his personal life in public. So much for "different cultures", I said to myself, and kept silent, retaining an unsympathetic look. As for him, it seemed as if he were searching for some salient example to prove his point, but then he looked as if he had given up the attempt.

Eventually I told him that I rarely spoke Arabic. Ali kept switching from Arabic to English, and I thought it was a good opportunity to assert my distance. But Ali didn't take the hint.

"Why?" he asked. "I thought London was full of Arabs."

"Yes, but I prefer to speak to them in English," I said.

"That's weird, man!" he replied, in English.

"No, not weird," I said, "I just enjoy the feeling of anonymity. Besides, speaking in Arabic would compel me

139

to accept assumptions and values which I no longer hold."

"How do you mean, man?" he asked.

"I mean if, for example, you speak to a Lebanese waiter in Arabic, the next thing he'd start talking to you as if you and he belong to one tribe!" I said.

"What's wrong with that?" Ali asked.

"Well, it's not true, is it?" I said, "We don't belong to one tribe, otherwise we wouldn't be here."

"You take things too personally, man!" he said.

"Yes, I do!" I said and told him how for the last seven years I had been frequenting a Moroccan bakery, but without ever speaking to the people there in Arabic. They had often wondered about me and once or twice asked me if I were Cypriot. I said no, and they looked at me, waiting for me to reveal my actual identity. But I didn't. They looked disappointed at first, but as time went by they accepted it and, I thought, respected my desire for anonymity.

"That's weird, man!" he said. "I tell you what, you wouldn't get away with such a thing in America! If you don't talk to people, tell them everything about your life and your business they would think you were hiding something!"

"Is that true?"

"Yes!" he cried. "As for the Moslem community, they are nosier than proper Americans. If they don't see you in the mosque on Friday, they come to your house to find out what's the matter."

"What! Do you go to the mosque? Do you pray?" I

asked, and was astonished to hear him talking about the "Moslem community" and "the mosque" with such a familiar tone of voice.

"Of course, man!" he said. "I'm a Moslem!"

"Oh, come off it!" I said and laughed. "We've always been Moslems, but we never went to the mosque and were never religious."

"I'm not religious," he said, and looked surprised that I supposed he was religious. "I am just an observant Moslem. I only do my religious duty!"

Now I understood why he had refrained from drinking beer, I told myself. When I went to the counter to order some sandwiches I asked him if he wanted a beer with his sandwich and he said no. It was a decisive no. I could not help remembering those three students from "The Right of Return" organisation, the three who had ambushed and beaten me that night on account of my being a traitor. I thought of telling Ali about them, particularly about that time when I bought them drinks but it turned out that they were religious. However, the thought of Ali as a religious person made me doubt that he would be able to appreciate the joke. Regretfully, I said to myself, when people become religious they lose their sense of humour, especially if they are Moslems. And then, as if only to prove my point, Ali told me how he started to do the daily prayers and frequent the mosque. He said that in his first two or three years in America he felt lost, totally lost. But gradually he started making Arab friends, and in no time he became a recognised member of the Arab community. Then he started getting suspicious and worried. What if they found out that he had been an Israeli collaborator? Most of the people he knew were supporters of Hezbollah, and if they became aware of his life back in Lebanon they would make it extremely hard for him to work and live among them. Eventually, and on the advice of a friend who was aware of his story, he decided to talk to someone: an imam of a mosque who was close to Hezbollah. Ali confessed to him, explaining all the circumstances which had led him to become an Israeli agent. He told the cleric that he was ashamed of his action, and that he sought penance. The imam was an understanding man, Ali said. He assured him that nobody knew, and if anybody found out he would make sure that no harm whatsoever came to him. But he could not, he told Ali, help him to repent. He was in no position to consider him a repentant Moslem. You could only become a repentant back in Lebanon, or in any other Islamic country, he told him. He told Ali that whenever he thought of going back, he could provide him with letters addressed to a number of influential sheiks at whose hands he could repent and receive forgiveness. Then nobody would dare harm him or reproach him.

"And in a sense, I'm going back to repent, now!" he said. For a few seconds I thought he was only joking. I thought, actually I hoped, that he would burst out laughing. But he didn't. He's serious, I said to myself. That's what religion does to you. It deprives you of your sense of humour.

What Ali had told me, I thought, was an additional reason to stop discussing the present. Eventually, and after quite a few attempts from me to steer the conversation away from our present lives, we started talking about the past, specifically about that evening when the four of us were together for the last time.

"It was that evening when George tried to explain Heidegger's philosophy to us," I said to Ali.

"Yeah, the thing about Being and the world . . . "

"Being-in-the-world!" I corrected him.

"Yeah! And the other thing about the difference between . . . "

"The ontological and the epistemological!" I interrupted again.

He nodded.

"But he didn't succeed," I said.

"He was weird, man!" said Ali in English.

"Yes, he was a bit of a strange chap!" I said, also in English, and went on to tell him what happened later that evening, after he and Maher had left the café.

Ali didn't look too surprised about the way George had behaved when we were nearly caught by the Israeli patrol. He kept saying: "He's weird, man!"

Nor did he look too surprised when I told him what he hadn't known about Maher's kidnapping and murder. I had assumed that Ali didn't know who the kidnappers were, or why they had kidnapped Maher. He had gone to America before one of Maher's kidnappers was captured and made to confess. And when I told him what the captured kidnapper had revealed, he looked as if he had already been told everything in full detail. At first I thought that his parents must have written to him about it. But no, it turned out that his parents had never mentioned Maher in their letters. They had never mentioned anything about any of us. I then thought that it must have been his long life in America, which made him look upon everything that had happened in Lebanon as a minor episode in some past and now forgotten life. But that was not it either. If Ali's long stay in America had taught him anything, it must have been how to be more focused on private and personal memories. He was eager to know intimate details about our families. For example, what had I known about George's family? Nor was he less interested when I told him the story of my sister Amina. True, he looked slightly embarrassed, and occasionally uncomfortable, but that was probably because he felt guilty that he was being told what should have been kept a secret.

There was an unmistakable gleam of curiosity in his eyes. Strangely enough, I told Ali everything about Amina, but I refrained from telling him what George had told me about his family that last night we were together. I treated it as if it was still a secret to which I alone was entrusted. After all those years, I still treated some secrets of the past as secrets of the present. I could not help feeling uncomfortable about it. I had come to believe that whatever had happened in the past should be up for revelation and discussion, and it was because of such a belief that I had eventually gained the courage to make my own revelation, to tell Ali about the circumstances in which Amina died. Of course I had always waited for an opportunity to tell someone about Amina's story.

Unlike my parents and my brother Kamal, I had never considered what had happened to Amina a secret. I was always willing to explain how Amina had died, but no one had ever asked me. It seemed as if people were satisfied with the explanation my parents gave for the death of their daughter, or that they were happy with the explanation that they made up themselves – that it was my brother Kamal who had killed her. Amina's death was not considered a secret by anybody, I said to myself, and that was probably one of the reasons why I didn't feel any better when I eventually told Ali about what had actually happened. Nor did I expect to feel any better, given that for a long time the memory of Amina had ceased to be the burden it had been for some years after her death. To be precise, I had stopped thinking of Amina just one year after I had come to London. Her memory had become just another part of the past, which gradually started to appear to me as an unreal world.

It was then that I ventured to ask Ali if he had ever felt that the past was unreal. I had thought that if he too had experienced the same feeling, then it must have been something in the nature of the past rather than my own perception, the soundness of which I had occasionally questioned. I told Ali that up to the moment when he phoned me, ten days earlier, I had felt that the past was somehow unreal.

At first Ali was amused, but as soon as he realised how serious I was he acquired the look of someone who was considering the matter from more than one angle. As I realised later, he often took on such a look when he had to face a serious matter. Eventually, and as if he had reached a subtle conclusion, he said: "I don't exactly know what you mean by unreal, but we were there, and things happened to us and other people. It was real!"

He seemed hesitant, however. And for a few seconds looked as if he wanted to add something, but instead remained silent. His silence implied that he was waiting for me to respond, but I didn't know what to say. More to the point, how could I explain it exactly? And would he understand what I had in mind? Why on earth did I ever ask such a question? I asked myself and wished that I could change this stupid subject.

But suddenly Ali went on, saying that just as with events and people, everything was as real as anybody or any event that he could remember from a month, or even a week, earlier. "They were actual people and events," he said, slightly unsure if he was answering my question.

"Yes, I know," I said, "but how about it as a whole, as one world?"

"That's different!" he said, and continued in the tone of someone stating a mere fact. "As a whole or as one world it could sometimes appear like a world in a story – a linear story."

"Yes, exactly!" I cried, and couldn't help feeling surprised at how right he was. I myself had thought of such a thing but in connection to his life in America. Three days earlier I felt that his phone call had helped me to see the past as real again. I reasoned that Ali's long stay in America could not be summarised or related in a linear narrative. It defies the logic of story-telling, I had explained to myself.

And that is what has made Ali's life real, and what has also made the past itself reappear so real to me.

"But why was that?" I asked now, at Heathrow, somehow hoping that he would say something to confirm my earlier thoughts.

He didn't answer and instead looked at me as if he expected me to know the answer, as if the answer was common knowledge.

"Why? Really?" I asked again.

"Violence, man!" he said impatiently and in English.

"Violence?"

"Yes, violence!" he said. "It makes everybody and every event look as if it has only one dimension. Like in an action movie, people seem flat!"

I didn't quite understand what he was talking about, and somehow I felt that his attempt to give some kind of a philosophical explanation was not entirely genuine. He looked as if he didn't believe in what he was saying himself. He must have realised that it was pretentious of him to claim that he had an analytical capacity for explaining a matter such as the one we were discussing. He started to put what he was trying to say into a story, as it had been originally.

He told me that he had had a similar conversation with someone but with regard to a totally different experience. He said that once he was talking to an old Polish man who had lived through the terrible times of the Second World War in Europe. The old man, Ali said, kept referring to his life then as a long nightmare. Sometimes the man didn't believe that he had managed to survive it. Ali agreed with him that it must have felt like a long night-mare. But with one important difference, he added: a nightmare was unreal, while what happened during the war was obviously all too real. The old man objected. He said that both memories, the real and the dreamed, had the same unreal nature. He went on explaining to Ali that because people in violent times and places lived in con-stant fear and worry about their survival, they were reduced to mere survivors. In other words, they had become people who had no other concerns or interests beyond staying alive. And once a person's life was reduced to that, the old Polish man said, it lost its diversity; and without diversity there could be no proof of reality.

If people see the same way and think the same way and do the same thing, the old man told Ali, then how could it be proved that what they see is real, and not an illusion or just one big dream or a nightmare?

"I confess, at the time, I didn't get the point," said Ali. He did not understand what diversity had to do with reality, and on this very point he disputed what the old man was saying. So the Polish man tried to explain. Unless different people, people of different tastes and different ways of thinking, see the same thing from different per-spectives, he argued, there could be no proof that such a thing existed.

"It's for this reason," Ali said, probably drawing a conclusion from what the old man had told him, "that after many years actual people and events could look fictitious."

I wasn't sure that I altogether understood or agreed with

what either Ali or the old man had said. It sounded as if they were talking about a work of art, not about life itself. There was something in the argument that made life too neat to be real. That said, it was none the less an exciting idea. For a few seconds I wondered if I should attempt an essay on the topic, an essay that would explore the possibility of seeing a society, at one time or another, as a work of art instead of real life. I could connect that possibility to the modern political thought which advocated the plausibility of creating a society from scratch. An essay of such importance, I said to myself, dreaming, is bound to arouse great interest. Of course I knew very well that I would not a write a word of it, and I soon remembered how difficult it was for me to achieve anything. Suddenly I felt depressed and wished to end our conversation on this subject, or indeed on any other serious subject. Conveniently enough our meeting was drawing to an end. Ali's flight was due in half an hour, and I thought it was a good time to gently steer the conversation towards something lighter. I asked about the old Polish man, how Ali came to know him, and why he had stayed in America instead of returning to Poland.

"Was he Jewish?" I asked.

Ali was a bit surprised, and for the next few moments he made no answer. His face just displayed a look which suggested that he was forced to consider the matter. Eventually he answered in an irritated tone, "Yes, he was Jewish! But what's that got to do with it?"

I didn't know what to say. It was impetuously asked and I was worried that he might have suspected that by my asking I was, indirectly, but ironically enough, referring to his past as an Israeli agent. Though he was no longer ashamed of such a past, he didn't like to be reminded of it – and certainly not in an ironic manner. I wanted to tell him that was not my implication, but I thought this would confirm his suspicion, or any suspicion that he might have had, and I decided to remain silent until the sudden tension, aroused by my question, had gone. Both of us remained silent for a few moments.

"Yes, he was Jewish," Ali said after a pause, but this time calmly. "His name was Bruno. And he was one of the most understanding people I've ever met. It was he who helped me get over the grief and the guilt and the shame that I had felt since the day Sameh was killed. And do you know how?" Ali asked, looking at me straight in the eye.

I knew that it was a rhetorical question. Nevertheless, I asked "How?" and he looked pleased that I had. Old Bruno was not the patronising type, he told me. When he knew what Ali had been through and how he had been feeling about it all, he did not lecture him on how to forget and let go of painful memories. Instead he told him what he himself had been through in his long and pre-carious hideout during the war. He told Ali that he was able to survive only because he had had to do things that induced nothing but shame and guilt. He had to pretend all the time. Not only had he pretended to be a church-going Catholic, he told Ali, but also, and on more than one occasion, he even pretended to be an anti-Semite. It was only by knowing what Bruno had done in order to survive back in Europe that Ali managed to place what he himself had done back in Lebanon in the larger context of what had happened there. He consequently felt less ashamed and guilty, he said, with a slight look of satisfaction on his face.

"Bruno was the friend I mentioned before, the one who encouraged me to seek the help of the imam of the mosque in Michigan," Ali said. "He himself had to seek the help of a rabbi. He had felt, as I felt later, ashamed and guilty. He seriously believed that he no longer had the right to call himself Jewish, he told me. But the rabbi taught him to see what he had done in the larger context of the horror that had engulfed Europe. He made him realise that what he had done was beyond his will, and that it would have been arrogant of him to think that he could have acted otherwise without risking certain death, Bruno told me. So it was Bruno who advised me to seek the help of a cleric of my community."

Ali was clearly proud of Bruno, and for a few minutes, he looked as if he was trying to recall the picture of his old friend. "Poor man, he was excited when I told him that I came to America through Tel Aviv," he said in a voice so low that he sounded as if he was talking to himself. "He wanted to go there, to visit, but he died before he managed to fulfil his wish."

"But why didn't he emigrate to Israel in the first place?" I asked.

"It was easier for him to go to America, and he was tired and confused," Ali said. Then he added, in a tone of voice which implied that he was proud of his friend's attitude,

"Besides, he was not sure that it was right for Jews to go to Palestine!"

"Didn't he believe in his right of return to the promised land?" I asked seriously, and I was surprised that I asked this question in such a manner. I had meant it to be sarcastic, but it came out as a serious question.

"What? Poor Bruno," Ali exclaimed, "he didn't believe in the right to return anywhere."

Bruno didn't think that it was possible for people to return, Ali explained. He believed that people only moved on; even when they went back to the place of their birth and early life they were only moving on.

"'It's a one-way journey!' he told me," said Ali, "'As for those who claim to return to a place where they never were,' said Bruno, 'they are simply confusing the symbolic and metaphorical with the possible and actual.' He said that the Jews who went to Palestine, they didn't return but emigrated to Palestine. The idea of a right of return in such a case is, he believed, no more than a claim on the past – the near or the faraway past – and perhaps the only possibly legitimate claim for those who are faced by the inhospitality of the world. The idea of return is actually an attempt to escape the inhospitality of the present state of the world – the discrimination and persecution," said Ali.

I would have liked to have heard such an explanation before, at least before I had met those three students from "The Right of Return" organisation. I would have certainly told them that if Palestinians were demanding the right of return, which was what their organisation claimed, then that was because they were living in inhospitable places. And let's face it, I would have told them, the Arab countries are not the most hospitable places, especially for Palestinians. Of course they would not have understood, I told myself. I thought they would have accused me of shifting the blame on to the Arab countries in a way that served nobody but Israel, or "the Zionist enemy", as they would have put it. They certainly would not have accepted the idea that there is no such thing as the right of return. And I thought that the best thing was to write it all in an essay or story. Yes, I shall write it as an essay or a story, which I could call *The Illusion of Return*. I liked the title and decided that as soon as I got home I would write it down on a big sheet of paper and stick it to the wall. Or I could stick it next to that poster which claimed that there could be no peace between Palestinians and Israelis unless Palestinians returned, the one that I had vandalised to avenge being beaten by those three students. That would be my own poster and I thought of telling Ali about it. But now it was time to leave. The flight's departure was imminent and, what was more, each of us looked as if he wanted to be alone. Eventually we rose to leave. I stretched out my hand but he threw his arms around me, and we hugged.

"You must come and visit me in America!" he cried as he walked towards the departure area.

"You must come and stay with me here!" I said, but of course I didn't mean it. Actually I had a strangely consoling feeling that we were not going to see one another again. It all belonged to the past, I thought, trying to justify that ungenerous feeling, but I couldn't be sure.

It was funny to see Ali after all these years, I said to myself as I got on to the tube. I nearly didn't recognise him. He has changed a lot – and he's managed to acquire a foreign, an American, outlook, I should say. In spite of the painful memories, he still managed to be lively and easy-going. And we did indeed remember some painful memories.

I knew that by saying such things to myself I was only trying to mitigate the deep effect the meeting had had on me. It had left me with the feeling that I had seen a friend going to a party to which I was not invited, a feeling which I had suffered from an early age whenever I saw a guest leaving. And this afternoon when I saw Ali disappearing into the departure area, I felt abandoned. For a moment I wished that I was going with him. But I knew that the only thing I could do was to see my encounter with him as merely a meeting with an old friend. I thought that that would help me return to my normal life. That was the only kind of return I cared about, I said to myself in a further attempt to regain that usual sense of life to which I had become accustomed. Old Bruno was right, I said, there was no return; it was a one-way journey.

"Old Bruno was right!" I said out loud, resting my head against the back of the seat in the tube which was speedily wending its way back into London. Bruno was right, I thought, but I was not sure.